TEXT AND DISCOURSE ANALYSIS

TEXT AND DISCOURSE ANALYSIS

Raphael Salkie

London and New York

First published 1995
by Routledge
11 New Fetter Lane, London EC4P 4EE

Simultaneously published in the USA and Canada
by Routledge
29 West 35th Street, New York, NY 10001

Reprinted 1997

Typeset in Times Ten and Univers by Florencetype Ltd,
Stoodleigh, Devon

Printed and bound in Great Britain by T.J. International Ltd,
Padstow, Cornwall

British Library Cataloguing in Publication Data
A catalogue record for this book is available from the British Library

Library of Congress Cataloguing in Publication Data
A catalogue record for this book has been requested

ISBN 0–415–09278–7

CONTENTS

ACKNOWLEDGEMENTS

A number of people helped this book on its way. My grateful thanks in particular to Sonia Critchley, Dick Hudson, Ann Jefferies, Alison Love, Barbara Mardell, Andrew Morrison, Chana Moshenska and Jeremy Nicholls. Earlier versions of the book were tried out with students on the MA in Applied English Linguistics at the University of Zimbabwe in 1993, and on the first year of the BA Applied Language at the University of Brighton in 1994. Their responses led to many improvements. None of these people is responsible for any remaining shortcomings. Thanks also to Julia Hall, Alison Foyle and Emma Cotter at Routledge for their commitment and hard work.

The book is dedicated to my parents, Essie and Benny Salkie, who richly deserve any *naches* it brings them.

USING THIS BOOK

This is not a normal textbook but a workbook. It does not try to tell you lots of things about language as would a textbook. Instead, it tries to help you ask interesting questions about language – and work out some answers for yourself.

In this book you will be introduced to some tools for analysing one part of language – text and discourse. The information in the book is kept to a minimum, just enough to explain:

- what the terms 'text' and 'discourse' mean
- the kinds of issues text and discourse analysis deals with
- how to use the analytical tools that help to explore these issues.

The book contains some questions about language, and a lot of data: samples of language from a wide variety of texts for you to analyse.

The book is designed to be self-contained and if you are truly dedicated you could work through it on its own. You will learn much more, though, if you use the book as a starting point for more extensive study:

- Find texts of your own to add to the ones in the book. Look for a wide variety of texts – books, newspapers, magazines, comics, advertisements, letters, official forms, novels, poems. . . use your imagination. The examples in the book are all quite short, for practical reasons. Find texts of different sizes. Find more examples of the phenomena discussed in the book. See if the tools offered in the book work with your texts. They won't always: in what ways are they inadequate? How can you improve them?
- As you work through the book, read some of the books and papers listed in the 'Further Reading' section at the end of the book. Be critical: ask how the concepts and theories in these books help to analyse real texts for useful purposes.

- Discuss the exercises with other students and with your lecturers and teachers. There is often no one correct answer to a question (the answers suggested in the book are model answers, not 'the correct answers'): work together to think of a variety of possible answers, then evaluate them.
- Look for links (or discrepancies) between text and discourse analysis and other areas of linguistics such as grammar, semantics, pragmatics and conversation analysis.
- Think about how the material in this book could be useful in language teaching, or other practical fields.
- Criticise the book. Send comments and suggestions for improvement to me, care of the publisher.

INTRODUCTION

This book covers some basic ideas and techniques in the analysis of text and discourse. Text and discourse analysis is one area of linguistics, the systematic study of language. The best way to understand what text and discourse analysis is about is to compare it with another area of linguistics: grammar.

GRAMMAR

Grammar (or syntax, as it is sometimes called) deals mainly with the structure of individual sentences. For instance, the rules of English grammar tell us that if some English words are combined as in example (1) below, they form an acceptable English sentence:

(1) If you want advice or practical help with health matters, ask your family doctor, district nurse or health visitor.

The rules of grammar tell us that if we combine these words differently, as in (2), they do not form an acceptable English sentence:

(2) Visitor health or nurse district, doctor family your ask, matters health with help practical or advice want you if.

Grammar, then, is basically about how words combine to form sentences. Some people think that grammar is about how to write and speak properly, so that 'correct grammar' would have us say things like 'Whom do you want?' rather than 'Who do you want?'. But grammar in linguistics does not try to lay down how people *should* speak and write; it tries to describe how people actually *do* speak and write.

TEXT AND DISCOURSE

A text, or a discourse, is a stretch of language that may be longer than one sentence. Thus text and discourse analysis is about how sentences combine to form texts. Take these three sentences:

(3) It's practically impossible to restrain children when they get to grips with technology. Which is why the computer equipment used in schools has to be designed and built to a standard above and beyond the normal call of duty. A standard that's set by Research Machines.

Combined in this way, the three sentences fit together to make an acceptable text. It may not be a very interesting or exciting text, but it is certainly all right. As with the individual sentence in (1) it doesn't break any rules or sound wrong or give the impression that whoever wrote it hasn't learned English properly. Now let's combine the sentences differently:

(4) Which is why the computer equipment used in schools has to be designed and built to a standard above and beyond the normal call of duty. It's practically impossible to restrain children when they get to grips with technology. A standard that's set by Research Machines.

Now the sentences don't fit together in a sensible way. There's nothing wrong with the individual sentences (just as in (2) there is nothing wrong with the individual words). It's the way the sentences are combined which is wrong.

COHERENCE

In grammar we say that a sentence such as (2) that doesn't work is *ungrammatical*. In text and discourse analysis we say that a text like (4) that doesn't work is *incoherent*. One of the key issues in text and discourse analysis is to find exactly what it is that makes some texts hang together while other texts are incoherent.

COHESIVE DEVICES

If we look at examples (3) and (4), it's not hard to see what is wrong with (4). Most strikingly, the words *which is why* at the beginning of the second sentence of (3) refer back to the first sentence. In example (4), the same words are at the beginning of the first sentence – so there is nothing for them to refer back to. For this reason, example (4) gives us the feeling that we are in the middle of a text and that we have missed the beginning, while example (3) can stand on its own.

Another thing that makes example (3) coherent is the way the words *a standard* in the third sentence refer back to the same words in the previous sentence. When the sentences are rearranged in example (4) this linking of words doesn't work, because another sentence gets in the way.

We can see from these examples that a coherent text has certain words and expressions in it which link the sentences together. Expressions like *which is why*, and the use of repetition, are known as *cohesive devices*: they are like the glue which holds different parts of a text together. Cohesive devices are only one factor in making a text coherent, but they are a good place to start the study of text and discourse because they are quite easy to identify. Just as important in making texts coherent are the intentions, expectations and background knowledge of the text producer (the speaker or writer) and the text receiver (the hearer or reader). We'll look briefly at these factors towards the end of the book.

ANALYSIS, NOT PASSING JUDGEMENT

We have seen that grammar in linguistics means describing how people actually do combine words into sentences, without passing judgement about whether these sentences are 'correct', meaning 'socially approved of'. Linguists take the same kind of approach in text and discourse analysis. Our aim in this book will be to find out what it is that makes texts coherent. Whether these texts are eloquent, interesting or great literature is not our concern.

SOURCES OF DATA

The texts we shall use as examples in this book are mainly real ones (not made up specially for the book), and they come from a wide range of places, from washing machine manuals to advertisements to novels. We shall be looking at their structure and asking how they hang together, not passing judgement on their literary qualities. Those of you who are interested in good writing may well find some useful ideas, but that is not the main aim of the book.

NUMBERING

All the example texts are numbered in one sequence that goes right through the book. Outside the exercises the number is in brackets before the text: thus the four examples given earlier in this introduction are numbered (1) to (4) in this way. The first text in the next chapter will be number (5), and so on.

In the exercises, two types of numbering are used. Each text in an exercise is numbered in upper case letters (A, B, etc.). But in order to be able to refer back to texts later in the book, a number in figures is also given in brackets at the end of the text. Thus instead of saying, 'Look back at example C in exercise two from chapter 1', we can just say 'Look back at example (12)'.

TERMINOLOGY

A quick note on terminology. Some linguists distinguish between text and discourse, using *text* to mean what one speaker or writer says, while a *discourse* for them has two or more speakers/writers interacting. In this book the two terms are used interchangeably to refer to any stretch of language that may be longer than a single sentence, and which therefore may have structural properties which go beyond the scope of grammar. For the sake of simplicity we shall usually use the word *text*.

And now – let's get going.

PART I
LEXICAL COHESION

WORD REPETITION

1

In this chapter we shall look at how repeating key words can help to make a text coherent.

One thing that makes texts coherent is repeating important words. Look at this example:

(5) The descending sun is temporarily eclipsed by a huge water tower. Shadows play off the concrete embankments of the Los Angeles River and dance across the shallow trickle of sewage in its channel. A locomotive shunts a dozen containers of hazardous chemicals into a siding.

We are only five miles from downtown Los Angeles but have entered a world invisible to its culture pundits. This is LA's old industrial heartland – the South-east.

It's 4.30 p.m. Two workers are standing behind an immense metal table, partially shaded by a ragged beach umbrella. A portable radio is blasting rock and roll *en espagnol*, hot from Mexico City.

Each man is armed with a screwdriver, pliers and a hammer. Eduardo, the taller man, is from Guanajuato in North-central Mexico, and is wearing the navy-blue baseball cap favoured by so many of Los Angeles's illegal immigrants.

Miguel, more slightly built and pensive, is from Honduras. They are unconsciously syncopating the beat as they alternate between hammering, prying and unscrewing. Towering in front of them is a 20-foot high mound of dead and discarded computer technology: obsolete word processors, damaged printers, virus-infected micros, last decade's state of the art. The thankless task of Eduardo and Miguel is to smash up everything in order to salvage a few components that will be sent to England to recover their gold content.

Being a computer breaker is a monotonous $4.50-an-hour job in the underground economy. There are no benefits, or taxes. Just cash in a plain envelope every Friday.

Many words are used more than once in this text. The word *is* occurs ten times, *a* fourteen times, and *the* ten times. Although these words play a part in making the text coherent, simply repeating them is not what counts. Any text in English is likely to contain many examples of these words: they are sometimes called FUNCTION WORDS. On the other hand, the text contains certain words which are used less often than these but occur more than once: these are called CONTENT WORDS; we wouldn't expect to find them in every text, and they do help to make this a coherent text. *Los Angeles*, for instance, occurs three times (four if we count *LA*), the names *Miguel* and *Eduardo* each appear twice, and the word *computer* is used twice.

Function words

Content words

These are important words in this text. We can show this in two ways. First, if we had to give a summary of what this text is about, we might say something like 'Illegal immigrants working as computer breakers in Los Angeles', using two of the three repeated words we just picked out. And since Eduardo and Miguel are the people in question, we would expect the text to use their names more than once.

Second, we can show that if these words were not repeated, the text would make very little overall sense. If the second instance of *Los Angeles* instead said *New York*, the third *Aberdeen* and the fourth *Doncaster*, the unity of the text would disappear. The same is true if instead of repeating the men's names, two quite different names were used (e.g. *Alison* and *Kathryn*); and if the second instance of *computer* was replaced by *fish*.

This may strike you as a rather bizarre way of looking at text (5). Obviously, whoever wrote this passage repeated these words because that is what she or he wanted to write about. Why would they possibly mention Aberdeen, or refer to 'being a fish breaker'? But this is putting the cart before the horse. We are trying to account for the fact that text (5) comes across to us as coherent. No one told us in advance what the writer intended in this text: in fact, the only evidence we have about the writer's intentions comes from the words on the page. When you read text (5), your assumption that it was a coherent text was confirmed. It's possible to examine texts to find out why this is so, and that is what this book is concerned with.

1. Find the important repeated words and phrases in the following texts.

A. CRICKET AND HUMAN RIGHTS HEAD AGENDA
From Robin Oakley in Harare

A new friendlier style of Commonwealth heads of government meeting was promised yesterday. Chief Emeka Anyaoku, the Commonwealth secretary general, announced that the proceedings, which open formally tomorrow, will include a charity cricket match.

Promised participants include John Major, Bob Hawke, the Australian prime minister, Nawaz Sharif, Pakistan's prime minister and Michael Manley, the Jamaican prime minister.

But away from sport, there were signs that British hopes of improving the Commonwealth's human rights record may run into snags. (6)

B. It took me a long time to pick myself up after my husband left me and our two young children. I'm 28. Eventually, though, through friends, I met a man. He has asked me out but I don't know what to do. I still love my husband although he has said he doesn't love me anymore. How can I learn to be comfortable with another man while I still have feelings for my husband? – *Kathy.* (7)

C. 'Twenty-two,' I called out to Angelina as I started for the kitchen door. Before I reached it two more policemen stepped through. And the main entrance was blocked by survivors of the original four.

'Trapped!' I shouted aloud, then touched the sonic screamer in my belt buckle. A number of the diners screamed in response as the vibrations produced feelings of terror. Nice. In the confusion I would escape through the fire exit hidden behind the drapes.

Except this door wasn't the only thing the drapes concealed. Two more policemen blocked my way. This was getting annoying. (8)

D. About one hundred house fires a year are caused by irons left on. And that's a conservative figure. Which is why our Comfort 750 and Comfort 400 steam irons turn themselves off, after thirty seconds, when left face down. Why after thirty seconds, you may ask? Well, leave a hot iron on your best cotton shirt. It'll begin to burn after thirty-two seconds. (9)

2. In the following extracts some repeated words and phrases have been left out, except for the first letters. Try to work out what these words and phrases might be. What clues did you use to get the answers?

A. NSS OFFERS A S__ PROGRAMME TO DEAL WITH RISING C__

In the week that both the Conservatives and the Labour Party have unveiled new proposals to deal with the rising tide of c__, *New Statesman & Society* would like to outline its own, s__, solution.
1. Create a new o__ of leaving a motor v__ unattended in a public place. According to the most up-to-date figures for notifiable o__s recorded by the police, this could, at a stroke, put a stop to up to 28.5 per cent of recorded c__ – the 1.46 million o__s of theft of, or from, a v__. (10)

B. Not all s_ t__s are alike.
On the one hand, there are ordinary s__ t__s which are usually no more than minor irritations.
But when you have a se__ s__ t__, it can be a different story.
By se__ we mean when talking can be difficult, when it's hard to swallow, and when you feel as if there's a continual lump in your t__. That's when you need more serious attention.
And that's when you need Merocaine. Because Merocaine is a t__ lozenge with a difference. (11)

C. Anyone trying to push a boat over a dry, level beach meets with considerable opposition. The fo__ which tends to oppose every sliding movement between solids is called the fo__ of fr__. Fr__ is an important feature of everyday life. The brakes of a bicycle or car use the fr__ between fixed 'brake blocks' and the m__ wheel to slow it down. Of course this effect is not always an advantage. Fr__ between m__ parts on a vehicle is one of the main causes of wear. (12)

D. SAVING THE E__

If p__ were the only threat, the e__ might be safe. The ban on i__ sales achieved at the last meeting of CITES (the Convention on International T__ in Endangered Species) three years ago was an historic achievement. A t__ going back 1,000 years was stopped. A slaughter which had so accelerated that the African e__ herd was halved in ten years was brought to a close. Pessimists who predicted prices would spiral through an illegal i__ trade fed by p__ were wrong. Some poaching continues, but only in a small way. (13)

---

3. As well as repeating words, some texts repeat patterns of words. This is a common device in speeches:

> (14) The people of this country aren't stupid. They know when politicians are lying to them. They know when newspapers are not giving them the full picture. They know when company directors on huge salaries are trying to make them feel guilty for wanting a decent living wage. And they know when their schools and hospitals are falling apart for lack of money.

What is repeated here isn't just the words *they know when* but the pattern *they know when x is doing y*. The x and y change each time, but the pattern stays the same.

✐ Pick out the repeated words and patterns of words in these examples:

> A. Merocaine contains two carefully selected ingredients that provide powerful and rapid relief when a severe sore throat strikes.
> The first is benzocaine, a strong anaesthetic agent that quickly relieves the pain in your throat.
> The second is cetylpyridinium chloride, a powerful anti-bacterial agent that in clinical tests has been shown to destroy up to 99 per cent of bacteria in the mouth and throat. (15; continuation of example 11)

> B. The future of teaching will now be determined on a one man, one vote system. [Picture of smiling politician.] This is the man.
> A review body on teachers' pay and conditions will soon be appointed by the Education Secretary, Kenneth Clarke.
> It will consider only the issues chosen by Kenneth Clarke.
> Its proposals can be overruled by Kenneth Clarke.
> Changes to teachers' pay and conditions can be imposed by Kenneth Clarke.
> Guess who thinks it's a good idea? (16)

> C. Men of England, wherefore plough
> For the lords who lay ye low?
> Wherefore weave with toil and care
> The rich robes your tyrants wear?
>
> Wherefore feed, and clothe, and save
> From the cradle to the grave,

> Those ungrateful drones who would
> Drain your sweat – nay, drink your blood?
> (. . .)
> The seed ye sow, another reaps:
> The wealth ye find, another keeps;
> The robes ye weave, another wears;
> The arms ye forge, another bears.
>
> Sow seed – but let no tyrant reap;
> Find wealth – let no impostor heap;
> Weave robes – let not the idle wear;
> Forge arms – in your defence to bear.
>
> from Shelley, *Song to the Men of England* (17)

(In poetry, rhymes and repeated rhythms are another form of repetition which makes poems cohesive.)

---

4. Simply repeating words can sometimes not be enough to make a text coherent. We saw this in example (4) in the introduction, where the words *a standard* were repeated but the text was incoherent. Here is another example:

> (18) It's stuffed with packs of condoms and AIDS advice literature. An AIDS victim like Sonia needs help, not discrimination. Jesuits in Britain are leading the call for St Aloysius to be officially designated as the patron saint for AIDS sufferers. Our Buddy service, which supports people living with AIDS, has trebled in size in three years. Meanwhile, Northern Ireland is beginning to confront AIDS.

Each of the five sentences in this extract contains the word *AIDS*, but the text as a whole is barely coherent. In fact, each sentence comes from a different newspaper article about AIDS, and they are just strung together here at random.

✎ For each of the following words, try to construct a short *incoherent* text in which every sentence contains the word in question:

School
Fire
Shakespeare
Teenagers
Gratitude

Do the same for some words that you choose yourself.

USING SYNONYMS

2

This chapter looks at how synonyms can be used to make a text coherent. Using a different word class with a related meaning is another way of making texts hang together.

Instead of repeating exactly the same word, some texts employ a different cohesive device: they use a word and then use a synonym of that word. A synonym is a word that has the same meaning as another word. Actually, finding two words which have *exactly* the same meaning isn't easy: *asteroid* and *planetoid* are a possible example, and for some people the words *sofa*, *couch* and *settee* are exact synonyms. When we look at texts we can count as synonyms words which are very close in meaning. Here is an example:

> (19) 'The doctor told me I'd been working too hard and I needed at least six weeks off work to get my strength back.'
>
> Amanda's employer, however, was less sympathetic. 'My boss gave me an envelope and told me it was redundancy money – two weeks' pay – £280. I was shocked.'

The words *employer* and *boss* do not always have exactly the same meaning. They are very close in meaning, though, and in this example they refer to the same person, so we can call them synonyms. It can get boring if the same word is repeated, and this is one reason why synonyms are used instead. It would have been possible to use *employer* on both occasions in text (19), and it would have been equally possible to use *boss* twice. Using synonyms instead adds variety.

There is a feature often found in texts that is rather like using a synonym. Look at this example:

(20) In the third year you can develop these special interests in particular areas of the subject, and it is here
that the breadth of the department's expertise is
especially an advantage: we offer courses in a very
wide range of specialist options, including compu-
tational linguistics and sociolinguistics.

The two words to focus on here are *breadth* and *wide*. These are
similar in meaning, but we cannot call them synonyms, because
breadth is a noun while *wide* is an adjective. None the less, it is clear
that the two words are linked in the same kind of way as the repeated
words in the last chapter and the synonyms of this chapter. There
was another instance in text (5):

Each man is armed with a screwdriver, pliers and a
hammer. . . . They are unconsciously syncopating the beat
as they alternate between hammering, prying and
unscrewing.

The noun *hammer* is linked here to the verb form *hammering* (the
term *gerund* is used for verb forms ending in *-ing* when they
are used in this way). Likewise, *screwdriver* is linked to *unscrewing*.
The writer probably had a little trouble finding a verb form to
correspond to the noun *pliers*: *prying* is not a bad attempt. The point
is that the original nouns correspond to the verbs that come later.
As there is a change in the part of speech or word class in cases
such as these, we can refer to this cohesive device, rather clumsily,
as SYNONYMS WITH WORD CLASS CHANGE.

**Synonyms with
word class change**

EXERCISES

1.   Identify the synonyms and what we have called 'the synonyms
with word class change' in the following examples:

A. I kept turning, my rigid index finger extended, to catch
his corpulent colleague just behind the jawbone with
this deadly digit. (21)

B. Britain made a 'profit' of nearly £2.5 billion from the
poorest countries in 1990, according to figures
released today by Christian Aid.
  The income from debt repayments was that much
higher than the total expended on aid from all sources.
  Ten years ago there was a net outflow from Britain
to the Third World of £5.3 billion. (22)

C. Some aristocrats argue that their behaviour is bad
because of their position in society. 'I do feel confused
about my destiny,' admits Jamie Blandford. 'I have
always resented having my life mapped out for me.'
  Royal expert Ingrid Seward agrees that people in
high places attract more pressure. (23)

D. A group of Commonwealth human rights organisations, mostly African based, are presenting a radical set of proposals on human rights which they want the conference to adopt. The group advocates the setting up of a commission to report on abuses. (24)

E. So everybody runs in fear, abject to authority. And everybody who has any hope at all aims for the top floor where the chairman lives. He lives always at the top of high buildings, or in fortresses on islands in warm water. . . .

And it is very scary to be in such a position, so you have to keep securing it. . . . Power held and loved and cherished in the hands for no other end than itself, yes. Oh, eventually it dies, of course. It goes round and round, eating everything in sight. So, bloated and gutted, it topples over, unable to control its own swollen body. (25)

F. Most groundwater for domestic, industrial or agricultural use is meteoric groundwater, i.e. groundwater derived from rainfall. The word meteoric comes from the same root as 'meteorology' and implies recent contact with the atmosphere. As we shall see later, the chemistry of meteoric groundwater changes during its passage through rocks. The modification of meteoric groundwater in its passage through the ground is an important part of groundwater chemistry. (26)

---

2. When a text repeats words, it is sometimes possible to substitute synonyms instead. This example text is from Exercise 1 (text 6) in the last chapter:

CRICKET AND HUMAN RIGHTS HEAD AGENDA
From Robin Oakley in Harare

A new friendlier style of Commonwealth heads of government meeting was promised yesterday. Chief Emeka Anyaoku, the Commonwealth secretary general, announced that the proceedings, which open formally tomorrow, will include a charity cricket match.

Promised participants include John Major, Bob Hawke, the Australian prime minister, Nawaz Sharif, Pakistan's prime minister and Michael Manley, the Jamaican prime minister.

But away from sport, there were signs that British hopes of improving the Commonwealth's human rights record may run into snags.

Here it would be possible to replace the second occurrence of *prime minister* by *premier*, and the third by *head of government*. While this perhaps makes the text less boring, it is rather contrived. For the other repeated expressions, *Commonwealth*, *cricket* and *human rights*, no synonym seems to be available. (It would be possible to use *the organisation* instead of one of the instances of *Commonwealth*, but this is a superordinate term rather than a synonym (see Chapter 3). The text in fact uses *sport* instead of repeating *cricket* – another example of a superordinate term.)

✎ Using the other texts in Exercises 1 and 2 in Chapter 1, suggest synonyms instead of the repeated words. Discuss the effect this has on the text. Where no synonym works in a particular case, attempt to explain why.

---

3. Some words and expressions are synonyms because they refer to the same thing, but differ in that one is less formal than another. Here is an example:

> (27) Two more policemen blocked my way. This was getting annoying ... I was trapped. Every exit was blocked, and the minions of the law were advancing.
> 'It's not that easy!' I shouted. 'Better cops than you have tried to capture Slippery Jim DiGriz. All have failed. Better a clean death than sordid captivity!'

Register differences

The word *policemen* is the neutral, everyday word. *Minions of the law* is a formal word, while *cops* is a colloquial, informal word. The term used for differences of this kind is REGISTER DIFFERENCES: we refer to 'formal register', 'colloquial register', and so on.

It is in fact unusual to find words from different registers in the same text. In the example, *cops* is used when the text switches from describing events to reporting what one of the characters said. The use of *minions of the law* is perhaps intended to create a light-hearted, entertaining effect. Most often, substituting a synonym from another register makes a text sound bizarre. Consider this example:

> (28) 'Farewell, your majesty,' said the Duke. 'We shall meet again.'

Suppose we substitute expressions from a more informal register:

> (29) 'Ta ta, your majesty,' said the Duke. 'Be seeing you.'

The same strange effect results if we make an informal text more formal. Here is the original:

> (30) Harry looked at Paul. 'Who's the kid?'
> 'He's a vice cop, undercover,' I said.
> 'That Giacomin's kid?'
> I put my hands in my hip pockets. I said, 'What's your connection with Giacomin, Harry?'

> 'I got no connection with Giacomin,' Harry said. 'And
> I don't want you sticking your nose into my busi-
> ness, you unnerstand.'

Here is the same text with synonyms from a formal register substituted:

(31) Harry visualised Paul. 'Who's the young human?'
      'He's a vice law enforcement officer, undercover,' I
      enunciated.
      'That Giacomin's offspring?'
      I inserted my hands in my hip pockets. I uttered,
      'What's your connection with Giacomin, Harry?'
      'I possess no connection with Giacomin,' Harry
      mouthed. 'And I don't desire you insinuating your
      nostrils into my business, you comprehend?'

✎ Substitute synonyms from a different register for some of the
words and expressions in the following examples:

A. After a decade, the Southern African Development Co-
    ordination Conference (SADCC) is celebrating its sur-
    vival. At its inception in 1980, apartheid South Africa
    had other plans for the region: economic co-ordination
    for production and wealth in South Africa. The more
    crude expression of that plan, the Constellation of
    Southern African States (CONSAS), is defunct, but the
    idea continues to re-emerge under new guises as
    discussions about a free South Africa most often speak
    of reform, not transformation. In the meantime,
    SADCC, not South Africa, has formulated and imple-
    mented 20-year plans for co-ordination of transport
    and for other diverse projects such as a genebank for
    germ plasm and research for hybrid food crops. (32)

Model Answer:

After a decade, the Southern African Development Co-ordina-
tion Conference (SADCC) is having a wild party about its still
being here. When it kicked off in 1980, apartheid South Africa
had other plans for the region: economic working together for
making things, and oodles of oof in South Africa, etc. . . .

B. They don't pull their punches in Camden. The Cube DJs
    Angus and Chris take a ride on the music roundabout,
    spinning around from Indie to Hip-Hop as they play the
    faves from KLF and EMI to a cheerfully-packed crowd.
    A dancer-friendly new night where the soundtrack ain't
    all upfront dance and ain't all oldies. We're not talking
    party hats either. Fresh! (33)

C. If expanded at the present rate 500,000 settlers will migrate to the occupied territories by 1995. Such an influx must question Israel's negotiating bona fides. Mr Baker sensibly concluded that there would be more will for compromise if, after five years of Palestinian autonomy, both sides found they could co-exist. The Israelis have permanently ruled out an independent Palestinian state. Mr Baker would only speculate on something 'more than autonomy and less than statehood'. (34)

D. 'I prefer female bodies aesthetically,' Caroline was surprised to hear herself say.

'Who doesn't? Why do you think so much pornography and fine art features women's bodies?'

Caroline looked at Hannah. 'If you really feel that, why are you with a man?'

'Because I love Arthur.'

Caroline blinked, then blushed, then studied her snowboots. 'I see.'

'Choices.'

'Why choose?' asked Caroline. 'Why not have it all?'

Hannah shook her head. 'You must have more time and energy than I do, is all I can say, Caroline.' (35)

SUPERORDINATES AND GENERALS

3

In this chapter we examine how superordinate words and words with a very general meaning are used as cohesive devices.

Another way of linking words in a text and creating coherence is to refer back to a word by using what is called a SUPERORDINATE term. Here is an example:

Superordinate

> (36) Brazil, with her two-crop economy, was even more severely hit by the Depression than other Latin American states and the country was on the verge of complete collapse.

The link here is between *Brazil* and *the country*. Brazil is a specific instance of the more general word *country*. The general word is called the superordinate, and the more specific one is called a HYPONYM. So *Brazil*, *Vietnam*, *Germany*, *Morocco* and *Zambia* are all hyponyms of country: they are sometimes called CO-HYPONYMS.

Hyponym
Co-hyponym

Hyponyms can themselves have hyponyms, depending on how elaborate the relevant area of vocabulary happens to be. A very elaborate area is the classification of living organisms. Starting with the most general words, we can go down the hierarchy of terms, getting more specific at each stage:

> *Living organism* has as its hyponyms *plant*, *animal*, *bacteria*, etc.

Choosing one of the hyponyms each time, we continue:

> *Animal* has the hyponyms *reptile*, *amphibian*, *mammal*, etc.

> *Mammal* has the hyponyms *primate*, *ruminant*, *sea mammal*, etc.

15

Ruminant has the hyponyms *cow, horse, deer, goat,* etc.

If we had started with one of the most specific terms, we could alternatively (and equivalently) have said that *cow* has as its superordinate *ruminant*, which in turn has the superordinate *mammal*, which in turn has the superordinate *animal*, and so on. If you are familiar with mathematics, you may have noticed that the co-hyponyms of any superordinate are the members of the set generated by the superordinate.

In a text it is often the hyponym which is used first; the superordinate is used to refer back to it (see the first further exercise at the end of this book for some exceptions). This is true of text (36), and it is not surprising: if you came across the superordinate first, you wouldn't know which hyponym the text had in mind until it was referred to specifically. This is clear if we reverse the order of appearance in the example above:

> (37) The country, with her two-crop economy, was even more severely hit by the Depression than other Latin American states and Brazil was on the verge of complete collapse.

We do not know at first which country is meant here, and when Brazil is mentioned it sounds as if this is a different country from the one first referred to. A hyponym always has a fuller, richer meaning than its superordinate: the word *Brazil* tells us everything that *the country* does and in addition tells us *which* country. The usual pattern in text is for the expression with the fuller meaning to come first, followed by the more general term.

EXERCISES

1. Find the links between hyponyms and superordinates in the following examples:

> A. In 1295, Good King Vaclav II of Bohemia founded the town of Pilsen. He was certainly an affable old ruler and granted numerous privileges to the town's inhabitants. One of these being the right to brew beer. (38)

> B. Students' experience of French is broadened using state-of-the-art language learning technology. In addition to advanced work on French structures and usage, students learn how to handle different registers of French and to recognise non-standard varieties of the language, both spoken and written. (39)

> C. Paul went out the door. I backed out after him. The Bronco was right in front of the station. 'Go around', I said, 'and go fast. Get in the other side and crouch down.'
>   He did what I told him and I followed, backing, my

gun steady at the open door. Then we were in the car and out of the lot, and heading toward Brighton along Commonwealth Avenue. (40)

D. Ten solicitors are facing criminal charges of defrauding the legal aid fund, and a further 31 are under investigation.

   The frauds have been unearthed by a four-man Legal Aid Board team of three former police officers and a solicitor. The unit was set up in 1980 after spot checks revealed a number of cases of inflated or improper billing. (41)

E. Experiment with positions and movements that might feel good during labour. If you are having the baby in hospital the journey there can be uncomfortable unless you work out in advance easy positions in the car.

   Imagine needing to vomit, pass urine or empty your bowels and work out easy positions for these natural functions. (42)

F. On stage or screen there's no one more raucous than Bette Midler. The plain little Jewish girl from Hawaii is now one of the Walt Disney studio's biggest stars. (43)

---

2. In the examples that follow, the original order of hyponym–superordinate has been altered so that the superordinate expression comes first. Find the places where this has been done, and comment on the effect this has on the text when compared to the correct order.

A. The Department of National Parks and Wildlife Management has started dehorning animals to stamp out poaching of the endangered rhino. Poaching has been on the increase in Zimbabwe as the horn fetches high prices in neighbouring countries, and this is one of various measures that have been introduced to curb the menace. (44)

Model Answer:

The words *animals* and *rhino* have been swapped over. The original read: 'has started dehorning rhino to stamp out poaching of the endangered animals.' The swap breaks the link between the two words, so that as it stands, text (44) reads as if some other animals have been dehorned to protect rhinos (visions of antelope gangs poaching rhinos!).

B. What are the mental processes involved in using language? What is the role of language in society? How are second languages learned? These are some of the questions to which the subject attempts to find answers.

All students are given an introduction to the basic concepts and techniques of linguistics. (45)

C. 'Tell me – why did you leave the safety of the car and risk being killed? You risked everything, everyone, for the man's existence. How could one man's existence be so important?'

'You've just said it yourself. What else is there more important than one person's existence? That is all he is ever going to have. All that any of us will ever have. One single shot at life, with nothing before and nothing to come. What you see is what you get.' (46)

D. The leaders attending the conference will discuss possible ways to speed up progress towards democracy in South Africa. Chief Anyaoku, the Commonwealth Secretary-General, said that it might be necessary to invite a representative from South Africa.

He also said that the presence of the ANC president, Nelson Mandela, was quite important as he would brief Heads of Government on the latest developments in the country. (47)

---

3. In some of the examples in Exercises 1 and 2 from Chapter 1, and Exercise 1 from Chapter 2, it is possible to use superordinate expressions instead of the repeated words and synonyms that are used in those texts. For example, the first extract in Exercise 1 from Chapter 2 (example 21) was:

> I kept turning, my rigid index finger extended to catch his corpulent colleague just behind the jawbone with this deadly digit.

Here *digit* is used as a synonym of *finger*. A superordinate expression instead would be *part of my body*.

✎ Where possible, suggest superordinate terms in this way for the texts in chapters 1 and 2. Where it is not possible, discuss why not.

---

4. The extreme instance of the use of superordinates is found when a very general word is used to refer back. One such word is *stuff*, which is such a vague word that it can be used to refer to almost any concrete mass noun. (A concrete noun is one which refers to something physical: examples are *water*, *sugar*, *hammer* and *elephant*.

Compare this with abstract nouns, such as *sincerity* or *faith*. A mass noun is one which does not normally have a plural and which cannot have *a* in front of it: examples are *water* and *sugar*, as opposed to *hammer* and *elephant* which are count nouns.) Here is an example of *stuff* being used to refer back in a text:

(48) Poor old chap, he's on his last pins, thought the boss. And, feeling kindly, he winked at the old man and said jokingly, 'I tell you what. I've got some medicine here that'll do you good before you go out in the cold again. It's beautiful stuff. It wouldn't hurt a child.'

Another very general word which can be used in this way is *place*, as in this example:

(49) 'The girls were in Belgium last week having a look at poor Reggie's grave, and they happened to come across your boy's. They're quite near each other, it seems.'

Old Woodifield paused, but the boss made no reply. Only a quiver in his eyelids showed that he heard.

'The girls were delighted with the way the place is kept,' piped the old voice. 'Beautifully looked after. Couldn't be better if they were at home. You've not been across, have yer?'

Other words of this kind are *creature* for animals (sometimes also for people); *person* and *people* for humans; and *thing* for concrete count nouns.

✎ Pick out the general words in these examples which are used to refer back:

A. Ken Bates, the chairman of Chelsea, yesterday resigned his position as a member of the Football League management committee. His resignation followed the record fine of £105,000 imposed on his club this month for making irregular payments to three players. ... The formal announcement of the resignation came at a press conference after a two-and-a-half-hour meeting of the full management committee at the London offices of the League's commercial department. Bill Fox, the president, said: 'It was a unanimous decision and we are pleased the business has been settled.' (50)

B. About four years ago the British popular media suddenly discovered the silicon chip. Acres of newsprint and countless hours of air time became filled with elucidations on the new technology, some of them distinctly bizarre. It was all too clear that the writers actually understood little about the subject, and that the understanding they succeeded in imparting to the public was correspondingly less. Since then things have improved markedly and it is rare now to see such howlers as the Wirral Globe's explanation of a 16K RAM as a chip with 'up to 16,000 different uses'. (51)

C. The white prisoners had been jailed in Pretoria, the black prisoners on Robben Island. . . . One of the things that worried me was David's sweet tooth. We were not able to get any news about jail food but we heard that the sugar allowance was infinitesimal and no sweets were allowed. David was a big sweet eater. I made an appointment to see Colonel Aucamp, the head of security, to request that David be allowed some sweets. 'Ag, no, man!' he said. 'These guys are prisoners, you know!' (52)

D. Hope the hospital is taking good care of you and that you're not absolutely bored to death. Remember, it's in a very good cause!! I haven't been much help to your parents with having Robert, but hope to remedy the situation when playgroup stops, as they'll be able to play together in the mornings. (53)

---

5. Some very general words can have a slightly different function in texts. Compare how the general word *problem* is used in these two examples:

(54) Surveys show that one of the most common causes of absence from work is back pain. Four out of five people will suffer from severe and incapacitating back pain at some stage in their life. How does the problem first arise?

(55) Dear Mrs Roberts,
I thank you for your letter of recent date.
I was most concerned to read of the poor service you received from the RAC and I wish to apologise unreservedly for the inconvenience you have suffered and which has caused you to write to me.
It is certainly the RAC's intention that your expectations of service would be fully matched in every sense and accordingly, your letter has been passed to the appropriate Operating Division of the RAC so that they may investigate the causes of the problem.

In (54) the word *problem* refers back to one particular expression, namely *back pain*. In (55), *problem* does not have one expression that it is linked with. In the text itself we can pick out expressions such as *the poor service you received* and *the inconvenience you have suffered* as linked with the word *problem*, but the function of *problem* is wider than that here. The word basically means 'the issues that this text has just mentioned': it is a way of referring back to what the text is about, rather than to specific items in the text. Other words used in this way are *question*, *idea* and *matter*.

Indeed, depending on the type of text, words like *story*, *letter*, *paper* or *book* can be used to refer back to the whole of the preceding text. For example:

(56) If you have enjoyed reading this book, look for other thrillers by Robert Parker and find out more about Spenser, the thinking person's private eye.

✎ Find the general words along the lines of *stuff* and *problem* which contribute to the coherence of these extracts, and discuss how each of these words is used.

A. 'And what about interviewing, because you interview a number of politicians like, well, the Prime Minister or the Chancellor of the Exchequer. Is that an easy thing to do, and how difficult is it when you're interviewing people that you don't particularly agree with or who get difficult with you during an interview?'
(From an interview with Brian Redhead) (57)

Model Answer:
The word *thing* refers back to the content of the previous sentence in a general way, rather than to specific words. Its meaning is roughly 'interviewing important people'. Also, the general word *people* is used here instead of repeating *politicians*.

B. I called out the RAC recovery service this evening and was asked the standard details by a member of your staff. When she asked me for the road name, I gave the full postal address of the company, from where I was calling, and explained that we are in a cul-de-sac which has no road name, apart from the area (Burnt Mill) but that we are directly opposite Harlow Town station. However, she refused to send anyone out unless I gave the road name. After a pointless discussion, in which I continued to give the fullest details I could, but no road name since there isn't one, the woman hung up on me. (58)

C. You've just answered your own question. Yes, of course you still love him – although not in the romantic way you did at the beginning of the relationship. But you both have created a bond during your time together, and that won't just disappear. Feelings of love don't automatically guarantee that you'll find it easy to live with the person you love – a difficult idea for many of us to take in, but true nevertheless. (59)

D. While many outsiders still look at Africa and see subnational 'tribes', SADCC is creating a region – not one which will replace sovereign states, but one which is altering their economic context.

   For the countries of Southern Africa to define the region on their own terms will prove even more difficult. A leader in the formation of SADCC, Tanzania has for political and economic reasons linked up with Southern Africa. Zaïre, however, has applied for membership to SADCC and been refused several times, even though historical mining ties connect Shaba province to the region. For political reasons SADCC has so far rejected this legacy; only major political changes in Zaïre will change this situation. (60)

E. 'I mean you don't have anything to care about. You are almost completely neutral because nobody took the time to teach you or show you and because what you saw of the people who brought you up didn't offer anything you wanted to copy.'

   'It's not my fault.'

   'No, not yet. But if you lay back and let oblivion roll over you it will be your fault. You're old enough now so that you'll have to start taking some kind of responsibility for your life. And I'm going to help you.'

   'What's lifting weights got to do with that stuff?' (61)

F. If you take a handful of sand and look at it closely – preferably through a magnifying glass – you will see that there are numerous tiny openings between the grains of sand. Sandstone is merely sand that has turned into rock because the grains of sand have become cemented together, and most of the openings will usually have been retained in the process – it is as though granulated sugar had become a block of sugar. (62)

OPPOSITES AND RELATED WORDS

4

> This chapter deals with other relations between words. Some of these meaning relations can be classified precisely, but others are harder to pin down. All of them can be used as cohesive devices.

In the last three chapters we have looked at three kinds of relation between words: identity (i.e. using the same word again), synonymy, and hyponymy. Other relationships between words can also be used as cohesive devices. One such relationship is when two words or phrases are OPPOSITE in meaning. Here is an example:

Opposite

> (63) At least 125 people died of AIDS in Bulawayo between April and June this year, according to City Health authorities. . . . Out of the 125, 71 were males while 54 were females.

The words *males* and *females* are opposites. Using the two words near each other obviously enables the writer to express a contrast, but it also contributes to the cohesion of the text. The structure of the sentence plays a part here: when we read *Out of the 125, 71 were males while 54 were . . .*, we expect to find a word that will contrast with *males*. By creating this expectation and then satisfying it, the writer helps readers to navigate through the text – which is what cohesion is all about.

Words like *male* and *female* are opposites in two important ways. First, they are the only two possibilities: a person is normally either male or female, and there is no other alternative. They are therefore called BINARY OPPOSITES. Second, the distinction is clear-cut: normally someone can't be partly male or a bit female – you are either 100 per cent male or 100 per cent female. The opposition between the two words is ABSOLUTE. Words which are binary absolute opposites are said to be INCOMPATIBLE with each

Binary opposites

Absolute opposites
Incompatible

23

other. Further examples are *alive–dead*, *even–odd* (numbers), and *digital–analog*.

Other kinds of opposite words differ from incompatible opposites either by not being binary or by not being absolute. Where there are more than two alternatives, the opposition is not binary but MULTIPLE. Here is an example:

Multiple opposites

> (64) We were digging the last hole for the foundation tubes. It was hot and the going was slow through rocks and roots. I was working with a mattock and Paul had a shovel. We also had use for an axe, a crowbar, and a long-handled branch cutter, which we used on some of the roots.

Starting with the word *mattock*, this text mentions five different tools. Although the writer does not want to contrast the tools in the way that males and females are contrasted in example (63), a similar sort of expectation is set up: when we read *I was working with a mattock and Paul had a* ... we expect a word which is one of the multiple opposites of the same set as *mattock*, i.e. a tool. Because there is more than one alternative here, unlike in example (63), our expectation can't be quite as specific, but its cohesive function is the same in both cases. In the next sentence we also expect a related word when we read *We also had use for* ..., and sure enough we get more tools. The different tools here are co-hyponyms.

In other cases the opposites are binary but not absolute, as in this example:

> (65) The composition of living organisms is very different from their surroundings. Whereas the environment consists of relatively simple substances such as gases, water and minerals, living organisms are made up of very complex molecules.

The opposition between *simple* and *complex* can be thought of as a scale running between two extremes. Something near one end of the scale will be simple, something near the other end will be complex, but there is no clear dividing line in every case, and something can be more or less simple, more or less complex (as this extract shows when it says *relatively simple* and *very complex*). Pairs of words like these are called ANTONYMS, and they can be compared with the incompatibles that we saw before: unlike antonyms, there is a clear dividing line between incompatibles like odd and even numbers; and a number can't be 'relatively odd' or 'very even' (except in a different sense of 'odd'!). Other antonym pairs are *large–small*, *generous–mean* and *loud–quiet*.

Antonyms

Converseness

Another kind of 'oppositeness of meaning' is called CONVERSENESS:

> (66) The European Commission proposal, published next month, aims to promote equal treatment of the sexes

in the labour market by making it easier for both parents to work and care for children.

The words *parents* and *children* are converses, since if *x* is the parent of *y*, then conversely *y* is the child of *x*. Other examples are *teacher–student*, *above–below* and *buy–sell*. Because pairs of converses are used to express the same thing in a different way, they do not tend to appear near to each other in texts as often as the other kinds of opposites that we have looked at.

In some texts the kind of oppositeness is harder to pin down. Everyone would agree that *male* is the opposite of *female*, but it isn't clear that *paradise on earth* is the opposite of *a lot of drudgery*. None the less, the contrast and the cohesive function in the next example are similar to those we have just looked at:

(67)   Bette Midler treats Hollywood, and all that glitz, with extreme scepticism. 'There's this idea that Hollywood is a paradise on earth,' she explains. 'But it isn't true. Being a movie star is a lot of drudgery but no one ever talks about that.'

The same is true of *a small number of jobs* versus *a wide range of employers* in this example:

(68)   Until recently, linguistics and phonetics degrees were directly relevant to only a small number of jobs. This is now changing. The trend towards European integration, and the growth of Information Technology, is making graduates who combine language and computing skills particularly attractive to a wide range of employers.

When a text expresses a contrast, it isn't just straightforward opposites like *big* and *small* that you should look for. Whatever words the writer wants to contrast are potentially analysable as opposites.

Of course, opposites don't just occur when the writer wants to contrast things. Look at this example:

(69)   'I like the machine. I am rather picky but no one ever lost their cool. Courteous and polite all the way. Would I do it again? You bet.'

To lose your cool is the opposite of being courteous and polite. But in this example, we are told that no one lost their cool: the negative of one extreme reinforces the other extreme which follows. Negating one of the opposites serves to emphasise the opposite which is not negated.

EXERCISES

Incompatible

1. Identify the INCOMPATIBLE pairs of words here:

    A. While some markets have become closed to South
        Africa, the other countries of the region have opened
        new markets for their exports. (70)

    B. 'Everybody has left you alone all your life, and you
        are now, as a result, in a mess. I'm going to get
        you out of it.' (71)

    C. The teaching on the BA is in three broad categories:
        core courses, optional courses, and service courses.
        The core courses are obligatory and cover the central
        areas of phonetics, phonology, morphology, syntax
        and semantics. The optional courses allow for indi-
        vidual interests to be pursued: they are of two types,
        foreign language options and linguistic options. (72)

    D. Three different mineral supplements were offered to
        groups of female Mashona cattle. The experiment
        started in June 1971 with 24 heifers per group and
        terminated after the third calving in September 1974.
        (73)

**Multiple
incompatible**

2. Find the groups of MULTIPLE INCOMPATIBLE words and
phrases in these examples:

    A. Many of the solicitors were allegedly inflating the time
        taken to advise clients. They were also submitting
        double, treble or even quadruple claims for waiting
        and travelling time when attending court on behalf of
        more than one client. (74)

    B. And when we ask for a ban on herring trade, to
        preserve an overfished resource, we are told in no
        uncertain terms that the Third World has no right to
        tell the First World what to do about conservation.
        After all, people who killed all the wolves in Britain,
        very nearly killed all the bison in the US and pushed
        the great auk into extinction know all the answers.
        (75)

    C. Would you rather help a fairy make magic, gnomes
        dig for treasure, an imp be naughty, a witch make a
        stew or Santa Claus deliver presents? [from a chil-
        dren's book]. (76)

    D. Compulsory Shakespeare for 14-year-olds – an excel-
        lent idea. Now which Shakespeare plays might the
        government be thinking of: *Romeo and Juliet* (under-

age sex), *Titus Andronicus* (rape and mutilation), *Macbeth* (murder and possible child murder in the past), *King Lear* (breakdown of family life and physical mutilation), or *Antony and Cleopatra* (adultery)? [Letter to the *Guardian*] (77)

3. Identify the pairs of antonyms in these examples:

A. 'Paul,' I said. 'You see before you an example of the law of compensation. The little weasel is ugly and stupid and mean and he smells bad. But he's tough.'

    'You'll find fucking out how tough I am,' Harry said. 'You may as well stick that thing in your mouth and pull the trigger. 'Cause you're a dead man. You unnerstand that?'

    'On the other hand,' I said to Paul, 'I am handsome, good, intelligent, and sweet-smelling. And much tougher than Harry. Let's go.' (78)

B. 'Hear the other side,' said St Augustine. It's easy to say but difficult to do. When fundamental freedoms are at stake it's particularly vital to hear the other side. (79)

C. No one realised that Getulio Vargas would dominate Brazilian politics for the next quarter of a century, for nineteen years as President. From 1930–6 Vargas behaved more or less constitutionally, though he probably knew that absolute power was his if he really needed it. He limited the powers of the state governments and their armies, and strengthened the hold of the central authority. (80)

D. Britain's 'woppies' have never had it so good – and they are putting some pep back into the property market. A new generation of 'well-off older people' is facing up to retirement with more spending power than ever before. And they are increasingly demanding a new kind of home – privately developed retirement communities. The market for such sheltered homes is still quite small – but there is massive potential for it. (81)

4. As well as these quite specific relations between words, texts often involve relations of meaning which are less easy to define but still play an important part in creating coherence. Here is an example:

(82) About one hundred house fires a year are caused by

irons left on. . . . Which is why our steam irons turn themselves off, after thirty seconds, when left face down. Why after thirty seconds, you may ask? Well, leave a hot iron on your cotton shirt. It'll begin to burn after thirty-two seconds. (Compare example 9)

Apart from the opposites *on* and *off*, the related words that help to create coherence here are *fires*, *hot* and *burn*. What these words have in common is not a precise relationship but simply that they all have to do with the general area of heat and fire, which is what the text is about. Here are some more examples:

(83) The Trade Descriptions Act makes it an offence for a tour operator knowingly to publish false information, and a draft EC package holiday directive should tighten the law still further. Fine print get-out clauses have been rejected by the courts, but the Consumers' Association says most people still fail to get adequate compensation.

(84) I am a 32-year-old single woman, living alone. I was made redundant four months ago. Recently I have felt dizzy and nauseous every time I leave the house. Just going to the local shops has become a major trauma. What's happening to me?

In example (83) the related words are *Act*, *offence*, *law* and *courts*, along with *tour* and *holiday*. In (84) they are *dizzy*, *nauseous* and *trauma*, along with *leave* and *going* and *house* and *shops*. In these examples it is hard to say precisely what the relationship between the words is, but it is clear that the words come from the same general area of vocabulary, and that they help the text to cohere.

✎ Find the related words that contribute to coherence in these examples:

A. When we put our minds to designing the next generation of pointing devices, we started with our hands. It turns out that thumbs have over twice the muscle and agility of other fingers – which only go up and down. We tested dozens of prototypes. None beat the design that is now Trackman. (85)

B. Caroline closed her eyes and nodded. She grabbed a tissue as a tear rolled down her cheek. 'Damn it,' she muttered through gritted teeth, blotting the tears, her throat aching from holding them back.
'It's all right. Cry if you want to.' As Caroline blew her nose, Hannah thought about the different ways clients did this. Some used the same tissue time after time. Others took a new one for each bout. Some collapsed on the couch and sobbed; others reached

out for her. Some, like Caroline, ground their teeth and struggled against each tear as though it were a drop of corrosive acid. (86)

C. Although some of the illustrations in this book are taken from published material and are appropriately acknowledged, the great majority of the diagrams have been drawn by my wife to whom I am greatly indebted, not only for draughting but also for much help and encouragement in preparing this book. (87)

D. This unique course combines the study of foreign languages (French and Russian) with the study of linguistics. The course combines high academic standards with a 'professional' orientation.
 We believe strongly that students learn best when they are encouraged to take charge of the process themselves as much as possible. We therefore include a lot of seminar and tutorial group work so that students can learn from and with each other. (88)

---

5. Some words frequently go together as a set expression. For example, we often talk of 'bridging a gap'. In this example, then, we can make a good guess that the missing word will be *bridged*:

(89) The Israelis say that since the gap between the two sides is so wide, it cannot be _____ in one step, but only by building mutual trust through interim agreements.

Similarly, we know that what you usually do to a claim form is 'fill it in'. Hence the fulfilled expectation in this example:

(90) You will be asked if you want to claim for any adult dependants. If you do, you will be given a separate claim form. Fill it in and return it as soon as you can.

Some groups of related words have been used so often that they have become clichés. Using too many clichés can make for turgid writing, but used with care they can be an important cohesive device. Every text has to balance familiar things with new ideas. Too much familiarity and the text will be boring; too much novelty and it will leave the reader confused. Cohesive devices help to create familiarity.

✎ See if you can guess the missing words here :

A. 'Is that all?' I asked, eyebrows reaching for my hairline. My Angelina never ceases to _____. (91)

B. In the week that both the Conservatives and the

Labour Party have unveiled new proposals to deal with the rising tide of ____. .... (92)

C. .As most people in Britain take their water supplies for ____, it is unlikely that they would stop to wonder where the water was coming from until the day when it failed to arrive. (93)

D. Paint could be on the way ____ as a way of marking lines on roads. Federal highway engineers in the US are promoting a new material based on epoxy resin which is supposed to be more durable. (94)

E. Dunn & Co., one of the oldest names in menswear and now up for sale, has become the latest victim of the recession. Dunn & Co. is speaking to four possible buyers, all of whom are British and three of whom are retailers. Ronald Hale, Dunn & Co.'s chairman, said safeguarding the jobs of the group's 700 employees was a priority, but not all the interested parties are keen to buy the whole group and run it as a going ____. (95)

---

6. Identify all the different kinds of opposites and related words in these examples:

A. The concept of Active Birth is based on the idea that the woman in labour is an active birth-giver, not a passive patient. So instead of lying down for doctors and nurses to do things to you, you get into positions which you find comfortable and move around as and when you wish. This means that you are not restricted to a labour bed or even a birth chair but are free to move around on the floor, in the shower, leaning against the wall, the furniture, or your birth companion. (96)

Model Answer:

birth – labour (related)
lying down – moving around (incompatibles)
active – passive (antonyms)
restricted – free (antonyms)
doctors – nurses (related)
floor – shower – wall – furniture (related)

B: Last night the Social Democrats said goodbye with a final party political broadcast. It was a final punctuation on the 1980s.

The Social Democrats emerged because a number of middle-class Labour supporters could no longer stand the party as led by Michael Foot, but felt the Liberals to be slightly beneath them. They daubed their Volvos and set forth from their second homes as missionaries to the Home Counties and the New Towns. They scorned the jibe of 'Tupperware politics' and intoxicated themselves with 40 per cent ratings in the opinion polls and the fair-weather friendship of the London media. (97)

C. And death shall have no dominion:
Dead men naked they shall be one
With the man in the wind and the west man;
When their bones are picked clean and the clean bones gone,
They shall have stars at elbow and foot;
Though they go mad they shall be sane,
Though they sink through the sea they shall rise again;
Though lovers be lost love shall not;
And death shall have no dominion.

from Dylan Thomas, *And Death Shall Have no Dominion* (98)

D. Mass uprisings suddenly erupted in the western coffee-growing areas where conditions were most horrible. The upheaval was triggered when Martinez allowed the Communist party to run in local elections. After the Communists won victories in several towns, however, the Army prevented them from taking office.

The poor had little more to lose. Their leader was Augustin Farabundo Marti, whose name would be taken a half-century later by other Salvadorean revolutionaries. Marti had joined the newly formed Central American Socialist party in 1925. He did not lack passion, but when the opportunity arose in 1932, it turned out that his cause lacked organisation. Martinez's forces quickly disposed of the peasants and then slaughtered thousands of others. Marti was captured and shot, and as many as 30,000 other Salvadoreans were wiped out in a matter of days.

The bloodbath changed the mind of Washington officials about the general. Before the slaughter, the State Department had been adamant about non-recognition. Two weeks later it admitted that 'Martinez appears to have strengthened his position'. In reality, few of his political opponents remained alive. (99)

PART II
OTHER KINDS OF
COHESION

SUBSTITUTES

5

> This chapter looks at *substitutes* – special words like *one*, *do* and *so* which replace words that have already been used.

There are some special words in English which contribute to cohesion by substituting for words that have already been used. The most important of these special words are *one*, *do* (or one of the other forms of *do*, namely *does*, *did*, *done* and *doing*) and *so*. Here is an example of each of these words used as a substitute:

> (100) Some took the same tissue time after time. Others took a new one for each bout. (From example 86)

> (101) Trades Councils should ensure that the local branch of the National Union of Journalists is affiliated. Even if an NUJ branch rejects an approach to join one year, try again the following year and keep on asking the branch to join until it does.

> (102) 'Charlotte seems a very pleasant young woman,' said Bingley.
>   'Oh! dear, yes; but you must own she is very plain. Lady Lucas herself has often said so, and envied me Jane's beauty.'

In (100), one substitutes for the NOUN *tissue*. The word *does* in (101) stands for the VERB *joins*. In (102), *so* replaces the CLAUSE *she is very plain*. In each case the writer could have repeated the original expression instead: the substitute enables such repetition to be avoided. What the substitute means is: 'The noun (or verb, or clause) in question can be found in the preceding text.' Using a substitute thus creates a strong link between one part

Noun

Verb

Clause

35

of a text and an earlier part, and helps to make the text cohesive.

In this chapter and the next we will look in turn at noun, verb and clause substitutes. First, though, it's important to notice that the three words used as substitutes in examples 100–2 also have other uses where they do not substitute for anything, as in these examples:

(103) One and three make four.

(104) If you do the right thing you'll be fine.

(105) I'm so glad you could come.

There is no other word or clause that *one*, *do* or *so* is replacing in these examples. So what we need to do is distinguish carefully between the other uses of these words and the ones where they are substitutes. We'll start with noun substitutes.

NOUN SUBSTITUTES

Here are some more examples:

(106) Postmen or women who want to flex their muscles or build up their stamina will be able to use a new health and fitness centre being built specially for them in Clifton Road, Cambridge.
Head postmaster Mr Tony Begley was keen that Cambridge should have such a centre, the only one of its kind outside headquarters in London.

(107) In any event the concept that MyoD1 represents a 'nodal point' – a point of potential regulation – in the pathway of muscle cell differentiation is a valuable one.

(108) While many outsiders still look at Africa and see sub-national 'tribes', SADCC is creating a region – not one which will replace sovereign states, but one which is altering their economic context. (From example 60)

In (106) *one* replaces *centre*, and in (107) it replaces *concept*. In (108), however, *one* doesn't substitute for one word but for the two words *a region*, as you can see if you try to fit these two words in instead of *one*. This means that it is not strictly accurate to call *one* a noun substitute, since a noun is an individual word like *centre* or *concept*, not a pair of words like *a region*. In the next example, *one* replaces even more words:

(109) Two cholesterol information evenings being held at the hospital on 9 and 16 August are already fully booked. A further one will be arranged for the end of August or beginning of September if there is enough demand.

The point is that apart from proper names like *John* and *Susan*, most nouns don't occur on their own in texts. They tend to come accompanied by other words which are said to modify them, and are hence called MODIFIERS. If we start with the noun *school* we can add different modifiers as follows:

school	noun
the school	definite article (def art) + noun
the secondary school	def art + adjective (adj) + noun
the Leeds secondary school	def art + noun modifier (nm) + adj + noun
the Leeds secondary school with many students	def art + nm + adj + noun + prepositional phrase modifier

Modifiers make the noun more specific. If we don't have any modifiers we can only talk about school in general (e.g. *School is boring*). If we want to talk about a particular school, we use as many modifiers as we need to distinguish this school from all others. A noun together with any modifiers it has forms a NOUN PHRASE. We can use *one* to substitute for:

- **Just the noun:**

I left the school and went to the one up the road (*one = school*)

- **or the noun plus modifiers:**

I left the Leeds secondary school and went to the Bradford one (*one = secondary school*)

I left the Leeds secondary school with many students and went to the one with few students (*one = Leeds secondary school*)

I left the Leeds secondary school with few students and went to the Bradford one (*one = secondary school with few students*)

In every case, though, substitute *one* is itself accompanied by at least one modifier. This is because when we use *one* in this way we usually want to contrast a particular example of the noun with another example. We therefore have to specify the new example, and this means using modifiers. The modifiers may come before *one*, as in (107) *a valuable (one)*; or after *one*, as in (108) *(one) which will replace sovereign states* and *(one) which is altering their economic context*; or both before and after, as in (106) *the only (one) of its kind*. Notice also that if the noun (with or without modifiers) being replaced is plural, *ones* is used.

EXERCISES

1. Say what *one* or *ones* is replacing in these examples:

   A. A group of people marching on the road should keep to the left. There should be look-outs in front and at the back wearing reflective clothing at night and fluorescent clothing by day. At night the look-out in front should carry a white light and the one at the back should carry a bright red light visible from the rear. (110)

Model Answer:

The word *one* in *the one at the back* replaces (substitutes for) the word *look-out.*

   B. That Malaysian planning is politically motivated does not mean it is necessarily inefficient. Although a number of criticisms have been made about the performance of the civil service, its record in development administration is by no means a bad one when viewed in comparative terms. (111)

   C. Excess cholesterol enters the body through our foods, especially animal fats, and many people are still unaware of the ones they should avoid. (112)

   D. Attempts to introduce forms of workers' participation have often been problematic. The Indian case is a particularly interesting one because the history of these ideas in that country is a comparatively long one, going back to the 1920s. (113)

   E. There isn't always an obvious link between the materials you have and the syllabus in use. The link through language is the most obvious and most straightforward one to make if your syllabus is based on linguistic items such as language structures or functions. (114)

---

2. Sometimes you will find *one* on its own; that is, without any modifiers, as in this example:

   (115) A strategy that is used repeatedly for monitoring status and progress in yeast is that of combinatorial control. There are different types of such control, and we have already seen one: the formation of a novel regulatory species, a1–x2, by combining polypeptides.

It looks here as though *one* is substituting for the whole noun phrase *(a) type of combinatorial control*. But this is not correct. Where *one* is modified its plural is *ones*: we would say, for instance:

> *Leeds secondary schools and Bradford ones.*

In example (115), on the other hand, the plural wouldn't be *ones* but *some* or a number such as *two* or *three*: *... and we have already seen some/two/three* (not *... *and we have already seen ones*). What we have in (115) is the number *one*, not substitute *one* (we'll return to examples like this, and examples of the type *He smoked one cigarette after another*, in Chapter 7 on ellipsis). We can often use this test to see if we are dealing with substitute *one* or some other use of the word: usually only the substitute has the plural form *ones*.

✎ In these examples, say which involve substitute *one* and which have number *one*:

> A. All Microsoft applications work in a common way
> – so when you learn one, you've learned them all.
> (116)

Model Answer:

The word *one* in this example is number *one*. To show this using our test, we try replacing *one*, first, with *ones*, and second, with *some*. Thus we get:

> (i) *when you learn ones, you've learned them all.
> (ii) when you learn some, you've learned them all.

Clearly (i) is impossible, while (ii) is fine. This shows that we are dealing here with number *one*.

> B. Many people think that underground water occurs in vast lakes in caverns. They picture the water as flowing between lakes along underground rivers. Successful wells or boreholes, they imagine, are those which intersect these lakes or rivers: unsuccessful ones are those which only hit 'solid' rock. (117)

> C. As you know, we are already outgrowing our existing storage space in the village hall – and this is before we have spent any of our funds on toys and equipment!
>   We would like to buy some push-along/ride-on toys for the toddlers and one or two bean bags, and we have been offered an indoor slide. As there is nowhere in the hall where we could store such bulky items we would like to erect a shed in the village hall grounds or in the playing field. (118)

D. In the time that you take to read this sentence, three people will die because they do not have ready access to a safe and reliable supply of drinking water. According to figures recently issued by the World Health Organization, an average of 50,000 people die each day from diseases associated with bad water; that is, one person about every two seconds. The figures are a grim reminder of how much we need water. (119)

E. Millions of Britons will be losers because the Government has refused to sign the European Social Charter. All the other eleven Community countries are coming together to build economic success based on a well-trained workforce and good working conditions. Our Government is the only one out of step. (120)

---

3. Testing for substitute one by checking out its plural will not always work. There is another use of *one* which also has the plural *ones*, as in these examples:

(121) We have recently set up a new group in our small village. Until now we have had no facilities for the under 5s and this in a village which has no shop and a very restricted bus service. Our aim is to enable parents and their young ones to meet on a regular basis, providing our youngsters with a safe, caring atmosphere in which to develop their social skills.

(122) How shall we organise this picture so that we can all be seen? Let's have the tall ones at the back and the short ones at the front.

In these examples the word *ones* is a general word like *stuff* and *thing* which we looked at in Chapter 3. The general word *people* could have been used instead of *ones* in (121) and (122). But *ones* isn't *substituting* for *people* in these examples: there is no previous occurrence of *people* (or any other word for that matter) which *ones* is linked with. So the key point is that *ones* is not a factor in making these texts cohesive: that's the basic difference between substitute *one* and other uses of the word.

✎ The examples that follow contain various different uses of *one*. Try to say in each case how the word is being used. Some of the uses have not been discussed here: you may find it helpful to look up *one* in a dictionary.

A. As in most countries of the Commonwealth, Nigeria first began planning soon after the Second World War, with the Ten Year Welfare and Development Plan of

1946–56. This colonial planning, however, had major weaknesses, one of the main ones being the absence of planning skills within the ranks of the generalist administrators ruling Nigeria during that period. (123)

B. Although in some instances, particularly in the case of sensory systems that are relatively well understood, it may be possible to construct circuits that are reasonably accurate replicas of biological systems, more often one extracts only the basic properties of the nervous system and uses this information to guide the design of the computer. The hope is that if one is successful in identifying truly relevant properties, then the neural analogy should provide a valuable contribution to the design process even though the circuitry of the nervous system is not understood in detail. (124)

C. There was a pause, while the fly, seeming to stand on the tips of its toes, tried to expand its wings. It succeeded at last, and, sitting down, it began, like a miniature cat, to clean its face. Now one could imagine that the little legs rubbed against each other lightly, joyfully. The horrible danger was over; it had escaped; it was ready for life again. (125)

D. However, she refused to send anyone out unless I gave the road name. After a pointless discussion, in which I continued to give the fullest details I could, but no road name since there isn't one, the woman hung up on me. (From example 58)

E. We went up to the mountain one day, up to the top. We went straight away first thing in the morning so that we knew there was nobody down the slope because that was the most important thing – we didn't mind killing ourselves, but we didn't want to kill anybody else – and so we got to the top. (126)

F. All single honours students study one, two or three of the following languages: *Chinese*, English, French, German, *Hindi*, *Swahili* and *Swedish*. The italicised ones are taught from scratch. (127)

G. The weather did not favour them that day. During the crossing to Calais, the boat rocked mercilessly and most of the children were seasick. The only one who enjoyed the crossing was Ben, calm and cheerful as he admired the seagulls and chatted with the cabin crew. He tried to get a game of rummy organised, but no one was interested. (128)

H. When I'm a bit more organised I'll give you a ring so we can get together – perhaps an impromptu visit one sunny afternoon would be best – then A & Robert can let off steam outside while I breast-feed. (129)

I. Use the Green Cross Code. Check which way the traffic is going and remember that in one-way streets there will usually be more than one lane of traffic going in the same direction. Do not cross until it is safe to cross all the lanes of traffic. (130)

J. I could hear them thudding up behind me now – and I relaxed. From the weight of their steps they could only be police. Criminals might have given me some trouble. But the local police! I could polish off a squad before breakfast – and still have an appetite for lunch. The footsteps stopped as the burliest one appeared before me. I tensed as he reached into his pocket – then relaxed as he produced nothing more deadly than an ornate golden badge studded with precious stones. (131)

K. A crucial ingredient here seems to have been the involvement of more women, both as workers and as committee members. Thus, the shift from a top-down and male-dominated approach to a locally based one in which females were enabled to play a large part proved to be a positive one. (132)

L. Conditions in the refugee camps are bad because of overcrowding and poor sanitation. One aid worker we interviewed said that medical supplies and tents were becoming scarce, and that things would only get worse as the cold weather approached. (133)

MORE SUBSTITUTES

6

This chapter looks at the verb substitute *do* and the clause substitute *so*.

The verb substitute is *do* (cf. example 101). Since *do* is a verb, and an irregular one at that, it also has the forms *does*, *did*, *done* and *doing*. We'll use *do* to cover all five forms. Here are some more examples:

(134) Needless to say, some people object to this: they argue that we should never write 'river water' or 'soda water' as one word, and so by analogy 'groundwater' should be 'ground water'. They doubtless have a point, but if we never allowed change in the English language we would still be writing as Chaucer did.

(135) You've just answered your own question. Yes, of course you still love him – but not in the romantic way you did at the beginning of the relationship. But you both have created a bond during your time together, and that won't just disappear. [From example 59]

(136) By the way, I have never yet heard how these remote islands became attached to the crown of Narnia; if I ever do, and if the story is at all interesting, I may put it in another book.

In (134), *did* replaces the single word *wrote*. In (135) it replaces *loved him*, and in (136) *do* replaces *heard how these remote islands became attached to the crown of Narnia*. So just as *one* could substitute for

43

a noun, or a noun and some of its modifiers, it is clear that *do* can substitute for just a verb, or a verb and some of its modifiers.

CLAUSE SUBSTITUTES

Clause
Sentence

The word used to substitute for an entire clause is *so* (cf. example 102). (CLAUSE is used here to mean a combination of at least a subject and a predicate. A SENTENCE, which is the largest grammatical unit, may consist of one clause or many clauses.) Here are some more examples:

(137) I walked past them, letting my left shoulder brush J.D. as I went by. I walked around behind my car and opened the door.
      Henry said, 'We'll be watching you close, smart guy.'
      'I hope so,' I said. 'You might learn something.'

(138) There was also the policy question of whether or not there should be an attempt to restore the convertibility of sterling, and if so how. These issues were the subject of what came to be called the bullion debates in the years around 1810.

(139) On Tuesday he was dressed and brushed and allowed to cut back to the City for the day. Though what he did there the wife and girls couldn't imagine. Made a nuisance of himself to his friends, they supposed. . . . Well, perhaps so. All the same, we cling to our last pleasures as the tree clings to its last leaves.

If we spell out the full version of these texts, we get a clause in place of *so* in each case:

I hope *you'll be watching me close.*

and if *there should be an attempt to restore the convertibility of sterling.*

perhaps *he made a nuisance of himself to his friends.*

Notice that the clause which is substituted by *so* is not definitely asserted in these examples. Rather, the clause is DEPENDENT: on the verb *hope* in (137); on *if* in (138) and on *perhaps* in (139). If we change the context so that the clause is definite, we can't use substitute *so*:

Dependent

(140) I know that you'll be watching me close (*I know so).

(141) It was decided that there should be an attempt to restore the convertibility of sterling. Since this attempt was going to be made, the question now was how (*since so, the question now was how).

(142) Certainly he made a nuisance of himself to his friends (*certainly so).

Noun and verb substitutes are typically used when the speaker or writer wants to contrast two noun phrases or verb phrases which are partly identical and partly different. The substitute *one* or *do* is used to save repeating the identical part. In (100), for example, *the same tissue* is contrasted with *a new one*; and there is a contrast between different kinds of loving in (135) (not all instances of substitution involve a contrast, however; there is no contrast in (136)).

At first sight it would seem that clause substitutes can't be used to make a contrast, since they replace the whole clause. In fact, we can talk about a kind of contrast in such cases if we distinguish between the words in a clause and asserting those words; that is, claiming that what the words say is true. Using *so* refers back to the words, but not to the assertion, and it is thus not surprising that it should be used in, for instance, examples (137–9), where the truth of the words is made out to be open to question. In (140), if the speaker wanted to refer back to the words and indicate that she/he also supported the claim that the words were true, she/he could have said *I know it*. (This point is taken up again in Exercise 4, Chapter 8.)

✎ **EXERCISES**

1. Say what *do* is replacing in these examples:

  A. They stood up. Victor walked towards her and put his hand on her back. 'Honestly, Lorie, I wasn't meaning to be a pain in the ass.'
   'I thought you weren't going to call me that.'
   'I like it. Can't you be a little flexible too?'
   'About my name?' Men seem to think that they can name women as they please, just because Adam did. That way they give women the shape and function they want them to have. (143)

  B. Robert Orr-Ewing, responsible for Knight Frank & Rutley's lettings in Chelsea, admits that fewer Americans are coming over, but those who move here are renting, not buying as they did in the boom years of 1987 and 1988. (144)

  C. 'I want it all,' I said.
   'You always do,' Hawk said. (145)

  D. The competition resulting from an increase in stock (capital) raises wages and decreases profits. Thus the progress of the British economy since Henry VIII's time, involving as it did a secular rise in the stock of capital, had led to a fall in the rate of profit. (146)

  E. Outside the stable doors the circling voices were

> raised and peremptory, and Iestyn, wild with weari-
> ness and anger, roared back at them incoherent defi-
> ance. Then, blessedly, Susanna's voice soared above
> the clamour:
>   'Fools, do you think there's any power can sepa-
> rate us now? I hold as Iestyn holds, I despise your
> promises and your threats as he does.' (147)

---

2.   The verb substitute *do* is like *one* in having a number of different uses apart from its use as a substitute. Here is an example:

> (148) I dislike the fact the House of Commons in many
> ways is a very amateur place, I still haven't got a
> desk or a telephone, which makes it very difficult
> to work. I dislike the kind of 'clubby' atmosphere,
> it's a bit like a gentleman's club, and I really came
> there to do a job of work. There's an awful lot of
> backbiting goes on there, and I dislike that.

General verb

This example illustrates the GENERAL VERB *do*, which roughly means 'perform an action (on)'. Speakers and writers tend to use this verb when they can't be bothered (or there is no point) to choose a more precise one. You are unlikely to confuse *do* in this example with substitute *do*, but consider these examples:

> (149) You can format your floppy disks by using the
> FORMAT command (see Section 3). Make sure this
> is done before you try to save any data on the disk.

> (150) 'I like the machine. I am rather picky but no one
> ever lost their cool. Courteous and polite all the way.
> Would I do it again? You bet.' (From example 69)

> (151) Clark argued that the 'natural' rates used by the clas-
> sical economists were, in fact, static. Clark said that
> Ricardo had adopted a static method, but criticised
> him for doing so only unconsciously; a result of this
> being that Ricardo failed to distinguish sufficiently
> clearly between statics and dynamics.

> (152) Asked afterwards why he had entered the burning
> shop, Mr Handley said that he had heard the cries
> for help and hadn't stopped to think. 'I'd expect
> anyone to do the same for my kids,' he added.

In these four examples it looks as if *do* is functioning cohesively. But in each case, *do* comes with another word or phrase: we have *do this*, *do it*, *do so*, and *do the same*. In examples (149–52), we have general verb *do*, not substitute *do*, so the cohesive device here is hyponymy, not substitution (cf. Chapter 3). The word accompanying do also refers back to previous words, in this case by means of reference (see

Chapter 8). In these examples we thus have hyponymy plus reference, rather than substitution.

✎ Say how *do* is being used in these examples (a dictionary would be useful here):

A. I'm one of the four presenters of the programme. We have two presenters on duty every morning and the programme is on six days a week. The presenter's function is first of all to introduce the recorded items that the reporters have made overnight or the day before and then to do all the live interviews. (153)

B. She claimed that many soldiers and ordinary people were terrified about what was to come but were too afraid to speak out. 'People are terrified,' she said. 'They blame the leadership for not doing enough to protect them.' (154)

C. We got a bus to South Kensington and did the museums. The children loved it – they're not interested in old monuments, but they'll spend all day at the Launchpad section. (155)

D. After the ceremony we all went to the village hall for the reception. It was a wonderful do – smoked salmon and frankfurters for everyone, with warm rolls and crackers. And as much booze as you could drink. (156)

E. On the poll tax for the coming year, Mr Heseltine said that benefits and other forms of relief made possible a national average community charge payment of less than £300. He said that an extra £4.5 billion of central support for local authorities meant that they could do their work properly 'provided they continue to exercise due diligence in rooting out inefficiency and waste'. (157)

F. Claims by President Saddam Hussein to have a nuclear weapon capability continue to be greeted with the greatest scepticism, if not downright derision, by Western experts. The advanced equipment needed to not only build a crude atomic bomb but explode it with the precision required to do damage is still beyond Iraq's existing nuclear programme, it is claimed. Experts do, however, concede that the Iraqis might be capable of launching a radiation waste bomb which would carry a conventional explosive and could strike terror if launched. (158)

3. There is a way of distinguishing between the general verb *do* and substitute *do*. The general verb *do*, because of its meaning of 'perform an action', can only be used to talk about actions. Now there are many verbs which don't refer to actions but to states of affairs. Compare these examples:

(159) John owns three cars and Bill does too.

(160) John owns three cars and Bill | *does this too

| *does it too

| ?does so too

| *does the same.

The problem with (160) is that owning a car isn't an action but a state of affairs. So the constructions involving the general verb *do* won't work in this case. But substitute *do* has no meaning of its own, and can replace *any* verb (except the verb *be*). I've put a question mark rather than an asterisk in front of *does so too*, because not all varieties of English use *do so* in the same way: some speakers, particularly in America, would not use *do so* for states and would reject this example, while others use *do so* for states as well as actions, and find this example acceptable.

✎ Try to use substitute *do*, and then a construction with the general verb *do* like those in examples (149–52), to replace the italicised part of these examples. Does the distinction between actions and states explain your findings?

A. I want three mint humbugs, and Ruby *wants three mint humbugs* too.

Model Answer:

If we use substitute *do* we get (i); if we use *do so* we get (ii):

(i) ... and Ruby does too.
(ii) ... and Ruby does so too.

I find (i) fine, but (ii) sounds impossible to me. To want something isn't an action but a state of affairs, and this explains why (ii) is no good.

B. I know everything about you and Mary *knows everything about you* too.

C. I can't get this computer to work, and Paul can't *get it to work* either.

D. Paul came from England to France, and Joe *came from England to France* too.

   E. Jean-Louis comes from France, and Pierre *comes from France* too.

---

4. We noted in the last chapter that noun substitute *one* is typically used when two things are being contrasted. The same is true for verb substitute *do*. If you look back to the first three examples in this chapter, you will see that (134) and (135) involve a contrast, whereas (136) does not. If you try adding *so* after *do* in these three examples, you'll find that it works in (136), where there is no contrast, but not in examples (134–5), where there is a contrast. It seems, then, that *do so* can only be used where there is no contrast.

✎ Test this suggestion on the following examples:

   A. If you enlarge Notepad to its maximum size, the following document will be easier to read. To do so, click the Maximize button in the upper-right corner of the Notepad window. Or open the Control menu in the upper-left corner of the Notepad window and choose Maximize. (161)

   B. 'We haven't played anywhere near our best this summer, let alone in this game,' he said, referring particularly to much of the top-order batting. 'We will have to improve a hell of a lot to really threaten the West Indies, because they won't let us back in the game the way England have done.' (162)

   C. Squatting is most comfortable when you hold on to something firm in front of you, or when you are supported by two helpers, one at each side. When you first start squatting, do so for a short time only, and either wear shoes with low heels or slip a pillow under your heels to avoid putting strain on the Achilles tendon. (163)

   D. In an effort to cut car thefts, potential buyers are being urged by the Home Office to pay as much attention to security as they do to performance and looks. (164)

   E. If you want to get on a bus at a request stop, give a clear signal for the bus to stop and never try to get on until it has done so. (165)

---

5. We've been comparing examples of the general verb *do* and substitute *do*. Another tricky distinction is between substitute *do* and AUXILIARY *do*. There are some verbs in English which are called auxiliary verbs because their job is to help another verb. Examples are *must*, *is* and *have* in these examples:

Auxiliary

(166) (a) John eats lots of vitamins.
      (b) John must eat lots of vitamins.
      (c) John is eating lots of vitamins.
      (d) John has eaten lots of vitamins.

Auxiliary verbs can do four things that other verbs such as *eat* can't do:

(i) Move to the front in questions:

(167) (a) *Eats John lots of vitamins?
      (b) Must John eat lots of vitamins?
      (c) Is John eating lots of vitamins?
      (d) Has John eaten lots of vitamins?

(ii) Have the word *not* after them in negative sentences:

(168) (a) *John eats not lots of vitamins.
      (b) John must not eat lots of vitamins.
      (c) John is not eating lots of vitamins.
      (d) John has not eaten lots of vitamins.

(iii) Appear in 'tag-questions' like these:

(169) (a) *John eats lots of vitamins, eatsn't he?
      (b) John must eat lots of vitamins, mustn't he?
      (c) John is eating lots of vitamins, isn't he?
      (d) John has eaten lots of vitamins, hasn't he?

(iv) Be emphasised to emphasise the truth of the whole sentence, not just the one word:

(170) (a) *John *eats* lots of vitamins (only all right in contrast with, e.g., *drinks*).
      (b) John *must* eat lots of vitamins.
      (c) John *is* eating lots of vitamins.
      (d) John *has* eaten lots of vitamins.

In each of these four instances it's possible to use the appropriate form of *do* to make the (a) example work:

(171) (a) Does John eat lots of vitamins?
      (b) John does not eat lots of vitamins.
      (c) John eats lots of vitamins, doesn't he?
      (d) John *does* eat lots of vitamins.

The sentences in (171) involve auxiliary *do*. Now the general verb *do* is not an auxiliary, so just like *eat* it needs the help of auxiliary *do* in the four constructions of examples (167–70):

(172) Brian does all the live interviews.

(173) (a) Does Brian do all the live interviews?
      (b) Brian doesn't do all the live interviews.
      (c) Brian does all the live interviews, doesn't he?
      (d) Brian *does* do all the live interviews.

In the following examples, the first *do* is the auxiliary and the second one is the general verb:

(174) Just then the puppy from over the road came lolloping up the path, wagging his tail.
'Hello,' he said, 'why are you up there?'
'I'm baby-sitting,' said Teddy Robinson.
'Are you really?' said the puppy from over the road, and he stood up on his hind legs, trying to see inside the pram.
'Please don't do that,' said Teddy Robinson, 'I'm afraid you'll wake the baby.'

(175) Right at the last, when hope was almost gone, the Tories' Geoffrey Dickens succeeded. Imagine a combination of bellow and croak, and you have the sound to which throat trouble has reduced the massive member for Littleborough and Saddleworth. Yorkshire was the subject of the question, and Dickens forgot that. 'Is the house aware?' Dickens asked ... 'It's got to be about Yorkshire, that's the point,' Mr Speaker interrupted. ' ... that my son, Clive, has signed up for the Gulf ...' 'Did he do it in Yorkshire?' Mr Speaker insisted. '... in Yorkshire. And isn't that more commendable than a lot of the yellow-bellied Labour members who ...'. And the rest was drowned in uproar.

There are cases, however, where auxiliary *do* is used in ways very similar to substitute *do*:

(176) The proposed EC convention on immigration is clearly racist, designed to deter immigration from largely black and Asian countries by its visa proposals. The racist character of the proposals is underlined by the recent decision of the EC to waive visa requirements for some Eastern European countries. Refugee agencies also insist that the distinction between a political refugee, who has rights under international law, and an economic migrant, who does not, is becoming untenable.

(177) Mark Tully, the BBC's man, introduced us and said, 'Mrs Gandhi, you will remember me, I'm Mark Tully, you expelled me during the emergency,' and she looked at him and said, 'and I may very well expel you again Mr Tully'. Now you know those are great moments: to see people of that kind of power and character. When you write about them as a historian you write about them as if they don't exist any more, but it's not true, they do.

Example (176) can only be auxiliary *do*, because only auxiliaries can have *not* after them, as we saw. But (177) is not so clear. The way to decide whether this is auxiliary or substitute *do* is to ask what the full version would be. There are two possibilities:

(a) ... but it's not true, they do exist.
(b) ... but it's not true, they exist.

In version (a), the full version keeps *do* along with the repeated verb: this must therefore be auxiliary *do*, used here for emphasis. In version (b), the full version just has the repeated verb: we are therefore dealing in this case with substitute *do*. In (177) it is version (a) which is more natural, so we can call the *do* in this text auxiliary *do*. Notice that the same test works for (176), where the full form would have to be ... *who does not have rights under international law* – another case of auxiliary *do*. In cases like (177), the word *exist* has been left out after *do*: this is an instance of ellipsis (see Chapter 7), not substitution.

Sometimes it's hard to decide which full version is more natural. If we say:

(178) Martin doesn't drive a car, but his sister does.

Then the full version could be either ... *but his sister does drive a car* (hence auxiliary *do*) or just *but his sister drives a car* (therefore substitute *do*). Clear-cut decisions aren't always possible in text and discourse analysis, but that isn't a problem so long as you understand how to make the decision in the clear cases.

✎ Say whether *do* in these examples is the substitute or the auxiliary:

A. Make a note of the positions and movements you prefer, so that when the time comes there is little chance of getting stuck lying down on your back, or in one position which you dare not change either because your whole body feels too heavy or because you are afraid that the pain will get worse if you do. (179)

B. 'Roz needs to broaden her horizons. She's a clever woman, and I think she is wasted by staying at home. It's not that I don't appreciate the work she's put in for me and the kids – I do, very much. But I sense us growing apart because our interests are so different.' (180)

C. I spoke to an American reporter about the breakdown in relationships between media and athletes. 'What's the matter?' he asked. 'Don't these guys want to be rich and famous?' They do, certainly, but only on their own terms. Steve Ovett refused to speak to the Press for years, then he held a press conference to launch a new line of clothes. (181)

D. According to the programme, Johnson has directed Alan Ayckbourn's plays. Certainly, he narrates his tale in a way that that technical maestro might be proud to do. (182)

---

6. Like the other substitutes we have looked at, the word *so* has a wide range of uses. There is, however, a simple test for clause substitute *so*: if you can replace *so* by *not*, then we have a case of substitute *so*. In examples (137–9), we can say:

I hope not
If not
Perhaps not

Whereas if we take a different use of *so*, as in (183), we can't:

(183) Competition, they tell us, makes the world go round. As long as we each spend our time trying to knock lumps off each other, then, apparently, a great civilisation is assured. So work hard looking after yourself, tread on anyone who gets in the way, and we'll soon put the Great back into Britain. At least, that's what our masters would like us to believe.

Here, *so* means 'therefore', and replacing it by *not* isn't possible. We can say that *not* is the negative clause substitute, *so* the positive one. Just as with the test for substitute *one*, however, this test must be used with caution. First, the crucial test for clause substitute *so* is to see whether it is indeed substituting for a clause. Second, the test works with *hope* and similar verbs such as *suppose* (*I suppose so* / *I suppose not*), but does not work with *tell* (you can say *I told him so* but not **I told him not*). Third, sometimes you can replace other uses of *so* by *not* for the wrong reason, as in these examples:

(184) Well, Percussion actually covers over 650 instruments and I actually try and play as many as I can but I think even in my lifetime I don't think I would be able to come across them all, because there are so many and they come from different parts of the world.

(185) Paul ate a hearty lunch at midday and John did so later.

In (184), *not many* is possible, and *did not* is fine in (185) (note here that (185) has the general verb *do* with *so* while *did not* is auxiliary *do* with *not*). The best thing is not to use this test on its own, but only to verify a decision you have made on other grounds.

✎ In these examples, distinguish the instances of clause substitute *so* from other uses of *so*:

A. 'Marty, you are the third person this morning who has offered to disassemble my body. You are also third in order of probable success. I can't throw a baseball like you can, but the odds are very good that I could put you in the hospital before you got a hand on me.'
'You think so.'
'I was proud of myself. I didn't say, "I know so."' (186)

B. In the twentieth century the focus of exploitation has changed but exploitation itself remains. Capitalist society now tries to preserve itself with a precariously interlocking and frantically stimulated system of greeds and so it encourages people to think of themselves primarily as consumers living in a consumer society. (187)

C. Plan your travelling to include plenty of opportunities to get up and stretch stiff joints. Don't expect to make a quick eight-hour car trip with only one stop for lunch. Plan in other stretching rests. On a train or plane make sure to walk in the aisle with your child every hour or so. (188)

D. The sparrow perched on the edge of the pram and stared down into the baby's open mouth. Then he turned to Teddy Robinson.
'That baby's hungry,' chirped the sparrow. 'Look, his beak is wide open.'
'Do you really think so?' said Teddy Robinson. (189)

E. If your network is loaded in the upper-memory region between 640K and 1 megabyte, you might have problems running Windows. If so, try loading the network in conventional memory. (190)

F. Direct radiometric age determination of Phanerozoic carbonates has been a long-standing problem in geochronology. Rb-Sr and K-Ar dating schemes, commonly used to constrain the chronology of Phanerozoic sediments, have so far proved to be unsuccessful in dating these rocks because of their poor enrichment in radiogenic ^{87}Sr and ^{40}Ar and also because of analytical difficulties. (191)

---

7. Because they have so many uses, the words *one*, *do* and *so* often occur many times in a single text. Here is an example for *do*:

(192) 'In effect your ex-husband is being asked to do you a favour. Does he know that?'
'I don't see. . .'

'He doesn't, does he? He thinks you've just been beaten down and have given up.'

She shrugged.

'What do you suppose he'll do when he finds out he's doing you a favour?'

'What do you mean?'

'I mean he's spent the last six months trying to get the kid away from you because he thought you wanted to keep him, and you've spent the last six months trying to keep him from getting the kid because you thought he wanted him. But he doesn't and you don't.'

Try to find other texts containing several examples of *one*, *do* and *so*. Invent some yourself: see how many times you can use these words in ten lines. (*Hint*: look up the words in a dictionary to find more uses than the ones discussed in the last two chapters.)

7 ELLIPSIS

In certain contexts it is possible to leave out a word or phrase rather than repeating it. This device is called *ellipsis*, and this chapter looks at the conditions under which it is possible.

A common cohesive device in texts is to leave out a word or phrase rather than repeat it. Here are some examples:

(193) Both Mr Major and Douglas Hurd, the foreign secretary, are engaged in a damage limitation exercise, eager to ensure that the sanctions question does not come to dominate this meeting as it has dominated the last three <>.

(194) If aggression should instantly be punished, why was not a man, not a gun sent to deal with the aggressors in the occupied territories of the Middle East, Cyprus and East Timor? Our middle-of-the-road warmonger waves this aside. International force was not used in the past, he agrees. It should have been <>.

(195) To learn a new language you've got two options: either you study grammar, vocabulary and phonetics for months and months or you can go back to the way you learnt things as a child. A child learns to speak almost 'by chance'. He imitates his parents without knowing why <>.

In these three examples I have marked the place where words are left out with the symbol <>. It isn't hard to say which words have been omitted: *meetings* in (193), *used in the past* in (194) and *he*

imitates his parents in (195). Leaving out words in this way is called
ELLIPSIS, from the Greek word *elleipein* meaning 'to leave out' (not
to be confused with 'ellipse', the geometric shape).

This doesn't mean that every time a text leaves things unexpressed
we have a case of ellipsis. Compare the previous three examples
with this one:

> (196) The Chairman reminded the Board that the General
> Conference had requested the Informal Working
> Group to continue its work with a view to reaching
> consensus on arrangements for the future financing
> of safeguards, and to report its conclusions through
> the Board to the General Conference at its thirty-
> fifth regular session.

Without further information, we can't tell from this text who the
chairman is, or which board, general conference, informal working
group or safeguards are being referred to. But this text is not elliptical, since though it requires *background knowledge* to make sense
of it, it doesn't require *preceding text*. That's the crucial difference
between this text and examples (193–5), where we have ellipsis. In
fact, ellipsis is very like substitution, since both involve referring
back to something earlier in the text. Whereas in substitution a
particular word refers back, in ellipsis there is a 'gap' in the text
which refers back. And like substitution, we can distinguish noun,
verb and clause ellipsis.

In Chapter 5 we saw that a noun and its modifiers together form a
noun phrase. An example was:

**NOUN
ELLIPSIS**

> The Leeds secondary school with many students.

The : definite article
Leeds : noun modifier
secondary : adjective modifier
school : noun
with many students : prepositional phrase modifier

With ellipsis we need to be more specific about the kind of modifier that allows ellipsis of the rest of the noun phrase after it. For
instance, instead of an article such as *the*, a noun phrase may begin
with a word such as *some*, *other(s)*, or *all*. After these words, the
whole of the rest of the noun phrase can be left out – if, of course,
the preceding text makes it clear what is meant:

> (197) Three hundred general practices will also manage
> their own budgets from April, though details have
> yet to be announced. Like their trust counterparts,
> their main motive for seeking autonomy is to
> improve the services they offer to patients. Such
> doctors tend to be the most innovative in their

fields. Some <> might opt out of the National Health Service altogether if, as Labour has promised, the whole policy were scrapped.

(198) The National Union of Teachers has sent guidelines to every school in England and Wales, suggesting ways of supporting pupils under stress. A number of education authorities have already issued their own advice. . . . Authorities that have issued advice to schools include Hertfordshire and Bradford. Others <>, like Tower Hamlets in east London, are intending to follow suit, although all <> will leave the detailed implementation of any policy to the schools.

It is also common to have ellipsis after numbers. Example (193) has ellipsis after the cardinal number *three*. Here is an example with an ordinal number (*first*, *second*, etc.):

(199) If it feels safer, let your new friend know that you feel cautious about relationships at present and ask him to be supportive. Many people still have feelings for a former partner while they are getting involved with a second. There's nothing odd about it.

Comparative and superlative forms of adjectives can have ellipsis after them, whether they are formed by putting *-er* and *-est* on the end or by using *more* and *most*:

(200) After making zany comedies, Woody Allen turned his attention to more serious subjects. Of all his films *Interiors* is the most intense, but not necessarily the best.

VERB ELLIPSIS

There are two basic kinds of verb ellipsis. The first kind, illustrated in (194) and again in (201), leaves out the verb and any modifiers to the right of the verb:

(201) David Fitzpatrick, who works for a charity as a lecturer in computing, has shared the care of his daughter Emma since her birth six years ago. He takes a lot of work home, but doesn't hesitate to take his daughter to work when he has to <>.

(202) Other domestic broils came at the same time to increase my chagrin. Madame le Vasseur, while making me the finest compliments in the world, alienated from me her daughter as much as she possibly could <>.

In (201) what is left out is the verb *take* and the words *his daughter to work.* In (202) the words *alienate me from her* have been omitted. If the verb is a form of *be* then the verb stays behind, and only the modifiers to the right are left out:

> (203) He leaned over the fly and said to it tenderly, 'You artful little b. . .'. And he actually had the brilliant notion of breathing on it to help the drying process. All the same, there was something timid and weak about its efforts now, and the boss decided that this time should be the last, as he dipped the pen deep into the ink pot.
>   It was <>. The last blot fell on the soaked blotting paper, and the draggled fly lay in it and did not stir.

In this sort of verb ellipsis, the word that precedes the ellipsis has to be an auxiliary verb like *can, could, should, have, be,* etc. (see the discussion of auxiliary *do* in the last chapter), or the word *to* as in (201), or *not* as in this example:

> (204) 'You know, I can't keep up with you, Caroline. Last I heard you were in hot pursuit of a man.'
>   Caroline frowned. 'Who says I'm not <> now?'

It may seem strange to call (203) an example of verb ellipsis, since the words left out are *the last (time),* and there is no verb here. The point is that ellipsis is always possible in English after an auxiliary verb. Normally, what comes after an auxiliary verb is another verb, as in (202). The auxiliary verb *be* is unusual in that it can have other words after it than just verbs. But whatever comes after *be* can be left out: the verb ellipsis process just applies more generally in this particular case.

In the second type of verb ellipsis, the subject and the finite verb are left out:

> (205) And what is the Prime Minister doing while all this is happening? I'll tell you what he's doing. <> Driving around in his flash car at our expense, that's what <>. Or <> chatting with his Cabinet friends about how ungrateful we are.

Here, the subject *The Prime Minister* and the finite verb *is* are left out before the words *driving* and *chatting.* It should be clear that the first kind of verb ellipsis is like verb substitution: in (202), for instance, the verb substitute *do* could have been used instead of ellipsis: *as much as she possibly could do* instead of *as much as she possibly could* <>. But the second type of verb ellipsis is quite different from substitution.

In this kind of ellipsis most of the clause is left out, and all that stays behind is a question word like *what* or *why.* Example (195) had

CLAUSE ELLIPSIS

ellipsis after *why*, and in (205) there is ellipsis after *what*. Here are two more examples with other question words:

> (206) Britain spends more than twice as much as France on prisons, and two-thirds as much again on private security officers. Clearly, different countries can do better in influencing the apparently inexorable climb in criminal behaviour: we need to look more closely at *how*.

> (207) 'I'm sure we'll find your mother,' said the man with the searchlight, 'But God only knows where.'

EXERCISES

1. The following examples contain various kinds of ellipsis. Say for each instance whether it is a verb, noun or clause ellipsis. For each kind of ellipsis make a list of the words or types of word that can precede the gap, starting with the ones already discussed above. Add to the list on the basis of the examples in this exercise, and then add to it any other words you can think of that behave in the same way.

> A. Many OAPs still have a hard time making ends meet – but some are sitting on a small fortune. During the last property boom they saw the value of their homes soar. (208)

> B. There are four newspapers specifically for Britain's 330,000-strong Jewish community. The Gulf war has put them in reluctant pole position for a huge international story. Yet all four share the same potential problem: they are weeklies, with deadlines that vary from early morning to late afternoon on Thursday. On the past two Fridays they have risked seeing their front pages made redundant by attacks on Israel. (209)

> C. I say that the critic new to the trade 'lowers his standards' when faced with a weekly fare of rubbish, and so he does; that is, he excuses the badness of the plays and marks them higher than he knows he should. Which is only reasonable while he does it consciously; disaster comes when he crosses the line into truly believing that the bad plays are really not bad at all. (210)

> D. The judge said that an employer's duty, under section 99 of the Employment Protection Act 1975, to consult a union when he was proposing to dismiss employees as redundant, arose when matters had reached a stage where a specific proposal had been formulated. Of two possible subjects of negotiation: whether there

were to be redundancies and, if so, how and on what terms were they to take effect, only the second was open for discussion, and the redundancies took effect on 31 December 1987. (211)

E. The PM has been wise enough to call for a 'bipartisan' approach, and the leader of the Opposition wise enough to concur. (212)

F. One female marine, Jacqueline Bowling, said: 'I do not think I have any more fears than the guys have. I think we have the same feelings.' Her husband, who serves at a post not far from hers, disagreed, and was unhappy to find that his wife had been assigned so close to the front. 'I guess that is where the male ego kicks in,' his wife explained. (213)

G. This form tells me that you want to vote by post, or get someone else to vote on your behalf, at elections for an indefinite period. It is for people who have a right to vote but who cannot reasonably be expected to vote in person because of the nature of their job (or their spouse's). Fill the form in carefully using *block letters* except for your signature. (214)

H. Telecom Security protects your home – 24 hours a day. As soon as an intruder is detected, an electronic signal is transmitted down your phone line to our Central Monitoring Station. We check if it's a genuine emergency. And if it is, we call for help in seconds. (215)

I. Sometimes he would have to take business trips, to Manchester, Birmingham or Leeds. Perhaps even to the Continent. He told her this with delight. Wouldn't it be wonderful if they could go together? He'd rent a car and they could drive up together. They'd be together, they'd see some of England.
     She drew back a little. 'Yes. I guess. Some time.'
     'Don't you want to?' Incredulous.
     'Yes, I'd love to. When I can.'
     'Well, why can't you?'
     'Victor, I have work to do. I have only a year here and a lot of material to get through.' (216)

J. 'I'm tired of bullshitting around,' Robert said. 'I don't want you comin' near April again. You understand?'
     'You really go to music school?'
     'You understand?'
     'I bet you don't. I bet you're a pimp instead.'
     Robert went inside the coat of his beige outfit and came out with a straight razor. He held it like he knew how.

'You better listen what I'm telling you, whitey.'

'Heavenly days,' I said, 'Talk about ethnic stereo-typing.' (217)

K. There is an embarrassing paradox in British tech-nology, in that much of the information classified as 'secret' by HM Government is exceedingly trivial while much that should be secret is not. Almost all the key advances in defence have come from contractors. The only way they can market their products is to produce literature detailed enough to convince the prospective buyer. Ivanov's major interest was communication satellites, in respect of which he was constantly being pressed to come up with something new. At one stage he even considered visiting the library of British Aerospace to gain (legitimately) information on British and American advances. Other targets were the big British defence electronics companies – Racal, Plessey, Marconi and Ferranti. He accumulated the equivalent of a suitcase-full of literature from each. (218)

L. Particles containing the b quark (bottom particles) are the heaviest found so far, some weighing in at around ten times the mass of the proton. (219)

---

2. The word *no* can be used as a noun modifier: we say, *There's no solution to this problem*. When there is ellipsis after *no*, it changes to *none*:

(220) I had just enough energy left to blow off the sheets, stall the boat and sit down behind the wheel, allowing accumulated exhaustion to envelop me. Twelve hours' sleep in the previous ten days, and none in the last four, had pushed my mental and physical stamina to limits I never knew existed.

(Notice also the ellipsis after *four*.) Why do we say that *none* is the form of *no* when there is ellipsis after it? One reason is that in other languages like French, the word would be the same whether it translated the full form *no sleep* (*aucun sommeil*) or the elliptical form *none* (*aucun*). Another reason is that there are other words in English which have different forms when there is ellipsis after them.

✎ Work out what these words are on the basis of these examples:

A. 'No one likes me,' I said, forgetting her problems.
Joan cuddled me close. 'Everyone loves you.'
'Just look at my frizzy hair,' I said to her.
'Well, gosh! Just look at mine,' she said, grabbing a bunch of her frizz.

'Yes, but yours is blond and mine's only brown and my eyes are only brown, too.' (221)

B. Frederic Raphael has been giving tongue (somewhat less coherently than usual) about film and theatre criticism, a subject on which I can claim to be an expert, having spent upwards of ten years in the live half of that extraordinary trade. Dear me; he must have got a very bad review for something or other, though it certainly wasn't mine of his translation of *Catullus*, which was a 'rave' so extravagant that it would have satisfied the most narcissistic actress on the stage, or indeed Freddie. (222)

C. Mrs Grimsley, who has three other children, told the *Leicester Mercury* yesterday that the action against Garylee's father was the only way to win compensation from his insurance company. 'We are both delighted for him because the money is not ours or anyone else's. It is Garylee's.' (223)

✎ In this connection, what is unusual about the words *his* (as used, for instance, at the end of example (224)) and *its*?

(224) This reason for the resolution I took, much stronger than all those I stated in my letter to Madame de Francueil, was, however, the only one with which I dared not make her acquainted; I chose rather to appear less excusable than expose to reproach the family of a person I loved. But by the conduct of her wretched brother, notwithstanding all that can be said in his defence, it will be judged whether or not I ought to have exposed my children to an education similar to his.

---

3. Look back at the examples in chapters 1–6 and see how many instances of ellipsis you can find. Good examples to start with are (186) and (86). You should be able to find at least ten instances. If you look at the discussion (not just the examples) in previous chapters you should find at least five more.

---

4. Look back at the examples of substitute *one* and *do* in the last two chapters. Try using ellipsis in these examples instead (that is, just leave out *one* or *do*) and see which of them work. Try inserting *one* in the examples of noun ellipsis and *do* in the examples of verb ellipsis in this chapter and previous chapters, and see which ones work and which do not. Can you arrive at any conclusions about the differences and similarities between substitution and ellipsis?

8 REFERENCE WORDS

> We turn now to some special words which need help from their environment to determine their full meaning. Because of this they are important in creating cohesion in texts. This chapter looks at the different words of this kind, and distinguishes them from substitutes.

Reference words

A very common cohesive device is the use of what we shall call REFERENCE WORDS. These are words which don't have a full meaning in their own right. To work out what they mean on any particular occasion, we have to refer to something else. They include the words *he*, *we*, *it*, *its*, *this*, *today* and *larger* in the following text:

> (225) A businessman would not consider a firm to have solved its problems of production and to have achieved viability if he saw that it was rapidly consuming its capital. How, then, could we overlook this vital fact when it comes to that very big firm, the economy of Spaceship Earth? One reason for overlooking this vital fact is that we are estranged from reality and inclined to treat as valueless everything that we have not made ourselves. Now, we have indeed laboured to make some of the capital which today helps us to produce things – a large fund of scientific, technological, and other knowledge; an elaborate physical infrastructure; innumerable types of sophisticated capital equipment, etc. – but all this is just a small part of the total capital we are using. Far larger is the capital provided by nature and not by man – and we do

not even recognise it as such. This larger part is now being used up at an alarming rate.

In the first sentence, when we come across the word *he* we know that we have to find the male human being to whom the word refers. The words *a businessman* tell us what the meaning of *he* is on this occasion. Similarly, the word *its* in *its problems* cannot be fully interpreted until we work out which 'it' the text means – in this case, *a firm*. The same is true for the other reference words listed above.

There are two ways to work out the full meaning of a reference word in a text. One is to look in the surrounding text, as with *he* and *its* in (225). The other is to look outside the text in the real world. The word *we*, for instance, refers to a group of people including the writer or speaker. To arrive at the meaning of *we* in a text, then, we need to know who the speaker or writer is, and which other people are included. In example (225) the writer seems to be including everyone in the world in this group. This isn't always so: in (226), *we* refers to a much smaller group, the writer and his fellow researchers (or fellow comedians):

(226) I feel that such hybrids as those made at the University of Hamburg (*Monitor*, 31 March, p.888) are hardly innovative. We have been involved in research of a very similar nature for some time, and although we are not publishing in such august journals as *The Phyrologist* you may be interested to learn of our most recent advance. Success in fusion of cellular material from B. stearo thermophilus and Canis familiaris metris optimi has resulted in our ability to culture, again in an isotonic monosodium glutamate medium, tubular elongated fruiting bodies. The technique is of course patented and the trade mark 'Hot-Dog' is being sought. (B. Whopper, Edinburgh)

When reference words refer to surrounding text, like *he* and *its* in (225), we can call this TEXT REFERENCE; when they refer to the real world, such as *we* in (225) and (226), we shall call it SITUATION REFERENCE. Obviously it is text reference which concerns us here, since it is this kind of reference which contributes to the cohesion of texts – so much so that we can ignore situation reference in what follows.

Text reference
Situation reference

It is important to grasp the difference between reference and substitution. Reference is a relation between the *meaning* of a word and its environment, where the environment can be the text or the real world. Substitution is a relation between *words*: a substitute such as *one* replaces another word or phrase. This means that there is no such thing as 'situation substitution' – or, to put it more concretely, a verb substitute like *do* can't refer to anything outside the text, but only to words in the text.

Another difference is that substitution is subject to tighter rules than reference: in particular, we can normally only use a substitute like *one* in a place where we could have used the original words instead. This is not typically the case with reference: it would not usually be possible to replace the reference item with the words that it refers back to. Compare these two examples:

(227) In any event the concept that MyoD1 represents a 'nodal point' – a point of potential regulation – in the pathway of muscle cell differentiation is a valuable one. (Example 107)

(228) A businessman would not consider a firm to have solved its problems of production and to have achieved viability if he saw that it was rapidly consuming its capital. How, then, could we overlook this vital fact when it comes to that very big firm, the economy of Spaceship Earth? (From example 225)

In (227) we could have used *concept* again instead of substitute *one*. In (228), on the other hand, the reference word *this* in *this vital fact* couldn't be replaced by some other words in the text. To know which vital fact the text means, we have to look back to the preceding words, but there is no question of replacing *this* by any of these words. To sum up: reference words are words looking for meanings; substitutes are words looking for partners. (What has just been said about substitution also applies to ellipsis, of course.)

PERSONAL PRONOUNS

The most common reference words are the personal pronouns *I, you, he, she, it, we* and *they*, along with their object forms (*me, him,* etc.) and their possessive forms (*my, your,* etc., and *mine, yours,* etc.). Since the first and second person pronouns *I, you* and *we* involve the speaker/writer and the hearer/reader, they are normally used for situation reference. The third person pronouns can be used for both types of reference. In speech these pronouns normally involve situation reference, while text reference is more common in writing. Here are two examples of *he*:

(229) [Watching a person on a film] 'Wasn't he also the chief baddie in the film *Hudson Hawk*?'

(230) Maurice Oberstein, the gravel-voiced boss of Polygram and, at 63, a veteran of the record industry, is particularly dismissive. 'Overnight sensations are crap,' he declares.

Here (229) involves situation reference, (230) text reference.

We have already looked at words like *mine* and *yours* in Chapter 7. Here is another example, which also contains two instances of *my*:

(231) Just after midnight on 16 January 1991 my son
woke me up to tell me the war had started. . . . But
what if this war goes wrong for the allies and
conscription is once more introduced? My son
fighting, perhaps dying, for his country? That is not
why I brought him up. To win this war, I am asking
other people's sons to risk their lives, yet here am
I saying, please God, not mine. . . .

It is clear that *my* involves reference, but what about *mine*? The
simplest thing is to say that *mine* here involves reference AND
ellipsis (of *son*). We saw in Chapter 6 that expressions such as *do it*
combine two forms of cohesion, hyponymy and reference. Here we
see that the word *mine* (strictly speaking, *mine* plus the gap after it)
combines two forms of cohesion. We shall see some more examples
of 'double' cohesive devices below.

The words *this*, *that*, *these* and *those* are called DEMONSTRATIVES.
This and *these* normally point to something nearby, while *that* and
those pick out something further away. In their cohesive (text reference) function they can be used with nouns, as in examples (232–3),
or without nouns, as in examples (234–5):

**DEMON-
STRATIVES**

(232) During the First World War, he told me, after he had
returned to South Africa, he set up a corrugated tin
roof in an alley off Smith Street. He ordered a small
quantity of drugs from England and then sold them
to the local retail chemists. . . . His orders got bigger
and bigger and eventually he ordered a large shipment of supplies from England. When this shipment
was under way, the Second World War broke out
and the drug companies could not send further
supplies to South Africa.

(233) Basically I play what we call tuned percussion,
which really entails xylophone, marimba – which is
like a xylophone except lower in pitch – vibraphone,
glockenspiel, tubular bells, and then you've got the
timpani or kettle drums and a vast amount of other
drums – and so basically the job of a percussionist
is to try and attempt all those instruments.

(234) Employees at the *Guardian* are hoping a meeting
next Wednesday between management and
national officers of the National Union of Journalists, Sogat and the National Graphical Association
will be successful. If not, the dispute will go to
conciliation. If that fails, the chapel will ballot on
industrial action, probably in early March.

(235) In the final year, a number of special option courses allow specialisation in areas of particular interest to the student. These normally include Syntax, Semantics and Pragmatics; Second Language Acquisition; Experimental Phonetics. . . .

In (235) we have reference plus ellipsis: the text could have said *these options*. In (234), we can understand *that* in two different ways: either as short for *that conciliation*, in which case we have reference and ellipsis; or as 'the fact that the dispute will go to conciliation . . .'. In this interpretation, *that* refers back to an extended section of preceding text, rather than one word. This is similar to the use of general words like *problem* and *book* in examples (55) and (56) (Chapter 3).

COMPARATIVE CONSTRUC-TIONS

General comparison

When two or more things are compared in a text, this can often contribute to cohesion. We can distinguish two types of comparison. In GENERAL COMPARISON, two things are said to be the same or different, without going into detail. Examples (236–7) illustrate sameness, and (238) illustrates difference:

(236) In our homes we associate the small screen with entertainment. We expect to enjoy the experience of viewing. Learners bring the same expectations to the experience of viewing video in the classroom. . . .

(237) House prices in the South are now 5 to 10 per cent below their peak of late last year, which reflects the fact that sellers are accepting more realistic prices for their properties. Such realism will be necessary to stimulate house sales over the next few months, Halifax comments.

(238) After a pointless discussion, in which I continued to give the fullest details I could, but no road name, since there isn't one, the woman hung up on me.
    I cannot believe that an employee of a Rescue Service can treat its customers in this way. I telephoned again ten minutes later and got a different person who was most helpful and arranged for someone to come out and see to my car. (Continuation of example 58)

Specific comparison

In SPECIFIC COMPARISON, two things are compared with respect to a specific property. One of the two things will be said to have more (example 239) or less (example 240) of this property:

(239) In language teaching we are accustomed to using dialogues which present very restricted examples of language. This is acceptable in the textbook, and can even be made to work on audio, but it is more

difficult when we can see real people in a real setting on video.

(240) The making and breaking of chemical bonds is associated with an energy barrier. At normal temperatures most molecules jostle with enough thermal energy to overcome this barrier. Near absolute zero, however, molecules have much less thermal energy. Therefore, even if two reactive fragments were side by side in a solid argon matrix, there would not necessarily be enough thermal energy to overcome the barrier and reform the precursor.

✐ **EXERCISES**

1. Pick out all the instances of text reference in these examples:

A. At one point the Brundtland report states that 'The loss of plant and animal species can greatly limit the options of future generations; so sustainable development requires the conservation of plant and animal species'. What, all of them? At what price? ... At another point the Brundtland report says that economic growth and development obviously involve changes in the physical ecosystem. 'Every ecosystem everywhere cannot be preserved intact.' Well, that's a relief. But how can it be made consistent with the earlier objective? Does it mean that it is all right to deprive some people in some parts of the world of a piece of their ecosystem but not others? What justification is there for this discrimination? (241)

> **Model Answer**
>
> The reference items are:
>
> > *them* in *all of them*;
> > *that* in *that's a relief*;
> > *it* in *can it be made*;
> > *it* in *does it mean*;
> > *their* in *their ecosystem*;
> > *this* in *this discrimination*.

B. We asked Ruby to describe for us what life was like in the African Rift Valley some 1500 generations ago. She replied that she had lived with a small group of about ten people: she indicated the number by holding up both hands with the fingers spread. They wandered the savanna during the day, looking for food, and sometimes met and socialised by the lake with other groups of hominids. It was during one such encounter that she met her mate, Klono. He wooed her by sharing with her a delicious baobab fruit. (242)

C. On the 29th December Daniel Deronda knew that the Grandcourts had arrived at the Abbey, but he had had no glimpse of them before he went to dress for dinner. ... 'I fancy there are some natures one could see growing or degenerating every day, if one watched them,' was his thought. 'I suppose some of us go on faster than others; I am sure Gwendolen is a creature who keeps strong traces of anything that has once impressed her. That little affair of the necklace, and the idea that somebody thought her gambling wrong, had evidently bitten into her. But such impression-ability tells both ways: it may drive one to despera-tion as soon as to anything better.' (243)

D. The friction involved in rolling is less than the friction involved in sliding. Hence it is much easier to roll a log along the ground than to drag it. This explains why the wheel forms a useful part of practically all land vehicles. For the same reason ball-bearings and roller-bearings serve to make movement easier and to reduce wear in machinery. (244)

---

2. Grammars of English say that demonstratives next to a noun can refer to people or things (*this man* or *that table*), but that demon-stratives on their own usually only refer to things (for instance, in *I don't like that*, the word *that* cannot refer to a person) (cf. S. Greenbaum and R. Quirk, *A Student's Grammar of the English Language*, London, Longman, 1990, p.120).

✎ The following examples don't conform to what the grammars say. Try to explain how the demonstratives in examples A–E are used. Text F has an example of *it* which is relevant here:

A. Ayleen pushed the woman into the room, trying unsuccessfully to hide behind her. There was a long silence. Finally the child stuck her head round and said: 'This is my mother.' (245)

B. I found out about people like Marx and Lenin. Lenin was a great humanist, both a thinker and an activist. I found his writing quite easy to understand. He explained society – how the motivation in our society is profit and how this means most people will live in poverty. He showed how to change this for the benefit of the majority. He explained that real power is concentrated with those who control finance. It was fascinating. We didn't hear about him at school. (246)

C. 'You see the man over there – the one with the wavy hair? Next to the woman with the laptop computer. That's the professor of chemistry.' (247)

D. Journalists on the *Daily Telegraph* received a 5 per cent rise, while those on *The Times* and the *Independent* have been given 8 per cent and 10 per cent respectively. (248)

E. Everyone always said I could have been a famous painter, like Rembrandt – I think he's the one that painted all those dark pictures, and they called those cigarettes after him because he was so famous. I liked painting flowers and pretty things, but Daddy wouldn't let me study it. He couldn't stand bohemians and people like that. I always felt I'd missed a big chance in life. (249)

F. Although neglected in England, Walras obtained influential followers in Europe, the most important being Pareto and Wicksell. It was Pareto who removed the theory's dependence on utility, arguing that the essence of the problem of economic equilibrium was 'the opposition between men's tastes and the obstacles to satisfying them'. (250)

---

3. The following examples contain some reference words not discussed above. Try to find them.

A. When the red man signal shows, don't cross. Press the button on the box and wait. The lights will soon change and a steady green man signal will appear; you may now cross with care. (251)

B. Another commonly accepted indication of intelligence is the way animals deal with the unpredictable contingencies of their world through learning; and it is here that our intuition tells us that we must be dealing with something very like intellect. After all, learning suggests to most of us some degree of understanding, some conscious comprehension of the problem to be solved. Alas, headless flies can learn to hold their legs in a particular position to avoid a shock, and even solve the problem faster than those still encumbered with brains. (252)

C. Ealing's chances in the first half were restricted to one penalty corner, and the Katie Dodd effort was cleared off the line by Karen Brown. From there, Slough poured on the pressure. Lesley Hobley always looked dangerous up front and Brown conducted play from the midfield. Her vision and control eventually earned her the player-of-the-match award. (253)

D. The main conservation achievement for which Ian Grimwood will be remembered is his successful leadership of Operation Oryx in 1962. This was the Fauna Preservation Society's expedition to the Aden Protectorate (now Yemen) to catch a breeding stock of the highly endangered Arabian oryx, a large and handsome desert antelope which did in fact become extinct in the wild ten years later. The three animals then captured, together with four more he later acquired by negotiation from the Riyadh zoo, became the basis of the very successful world herd of Arabian oryx located in the USA at zoos in Phoenix, Arizona, and San Diego, California. (254)

---

4. We said in Chapter 6 that clause substitute *so* is used just to replace certain words, while *it* is used to refer back to the words and the assertion made by using the words (cf. examples 137–42). For more evidence that this is correct, compare these two examples:

(255) Mary said that Britain caused the Second World War, but she couldn't get anyone else to believe it.

(256) Mary thinks that there is another planet beyond Pluto, but no one else thinks so.

In (255), *it* refers back specifically to Mary's assertion about the cause of the war. In (256), *so* refers back only to the belief that there is another planet, not to Mary's belief that there is another planet. If we had used *so* in (255) and *it* in (256) the sentences wouldn't have been quite right.

✎ Test this claim about the difference between *so* and *it* by replacing one by the other in these examples and seeing what happens:

A. Sidney shook his head at these developments and said sadly, 'I told you so. You watch, every time someone does a real job – a good job for liberation in South Africa, it will be called off on one pretext or another.' (257)

B. As soon as the words were out of my mouth, Edna looked at me in amazement.
'We-ell,' she said, drawing the word out, 'You said it – not me.' (258)

C. I was Daddy's favourite child. I'm sure I was. Daddy was very strict and when he hit us we knew it was for our own good. He hated punishing us and he said so, but we benefited from it. We all thank him for it now. (259)

D. 'Do you think you'll pass the exam?'
  'God only knows.'
  'Will your old man be angry if you fail?'
  'I expect so.' (260)

E. I lay there seething. Imagine inviting a woman into your bedroom, I thought, and then just falling asleep. He's all very animated and chatty when there are people around. He even put his arm across my shoulder on the way home. That's a come-on, isn't it? I felt insulted. My mother wouldn't have believed it. She'd often said to me, 'Remember, men only want one thing – they're all the same. And if you give it to them then they want it from someone else.' It was obvious she hadn't met a character like this. (261)

---

5. In many cases you can refer back to the same thing using *it*, *this* or *that*, with no difference apart from one of emphasis. This is true when the thing referred back to is an object as in (262), or previous text as in (263):

(262) Graham reckons that we should buy a laser printer. He says {it/this/that} will speed up our output enormously.

(263) My brother used to tease me all the time. I hated {it/this/that}.

✎ In the examples that follow, however, only one of the three words will do. Try to explain why this is so.

A. First you go into the hall, and then through a doorway into the living room, which sort of curves itself around so that it's not really a square room. It's maybe ten, twelve feet, but the width of it varies. (264)

B. <The writer is giving a chapter-by-chapter summary of his university dissertation, starting with the introduction>.
  Introduction: This traces the developments in dialectology in recent years. (265)

C. 'She's having a baby.'
  'How do you know that?' (266)

D. The B minor suite came floating up from the great

hall to the ears of the two men in the laboratory. They were too busy to realise that they were hearing it. (267)

E. 'I met her first at the pictures on Saturday afternoon when it was raining. It was an accident like. She was sitting next to me and she dropped her bag and I picked it up and she said thank you and so naturally we got talking.'

'And d'you mean to tell me you fell for an old trick like that? Dropped her bag indeed. . . . And when did all this happen?' (268)

CONNECTIVES

9

> Some words and phrases are used to indicate a specific connection between different parts of a text. We call such words and phrases connectives.

It often happens that two parts of a text are connected in meaning. For instance, in a story, the events described in one sentence often follow the events described in the previous sentence. Sometimes this connection may be explicitly stated in the text; or it may be implicit and left for the reader to figure out. Compare these two examples:

(269) I handed Paul the canteen of water. He drank a little and handed it back to me. I drank and hung it back up.

(270) Gooch can seldom have hit the ball more sweetly. He drove McDermott to the cover boundary off both front and back foot; he took three fours off Matthews in four balls; then he pulled Reid for four with a pistol crack to reach the elusive century.

In (269) we assume that the events happened in the order described, but there is no explicit indication of what came after what. In (270) the word *then* explicitly indicates the time sequence. We shall call *then* a connective: one of the words and phrases which indicate a connection between parts of a text.

Various kinds of words and phrases can function as connectives. They include:

- Conjunctions like *but*:

(271) It placed severe personal problems on me, but it was all worthwhile.

75

- Adverbs like *nevertheless*:

(272) It placed severe personal problems on me; nevertheless, it was all worthwhile.

- Prepositional expressions like *in spite of*:

(273) In spite of the severe personal problems it placed on me, it was all worthwhile.

The term *connective* does not refer to a part of speech (word class) like *conjunction* or *adverb*. It is because they all do the same job of linking parts of a text that we treat *but*, *nevertheless* and *in spite of* as connectives.

TYPES OF CONNECTIVE

It is useful to distinguish four basic types of connective:

1   Addition connectives (AC) (example: *and*)
2   Opposition connectives (OC) (example: *yet*)
3   Cause connectives (CC) (example: *therefore*)
4   Time connectives (TC) (example: *then* in (270))

Addition connectives

Here are some examples of ACs:

(274) If you happened to catch the January 1975 issue of *Popular Electronics* you were one of the lucky few to witness the debut of the personal computer. Impossible as it seems, a magazine with less than 10 per cent the readership of *Time* or *Newsweek* launched a technology race roughly parallel to that of the space program. It *also* launched a company that quickly took centre stage in the exciting new world of personal computing. The company was Microsoft, *and* the tenet on which it was founded was a simple one. To see a computer on every desk and in every home.

(275) Today, only forty-four inhabitants remain [on Pitcairn Island]. Conditions on the island have deteriorated, *and* their only contact with the outside world is via an antiquated radio link with the British Consulate in New Zealand *and* (weather permitting) two passing ships a year. *In other words* the Pitcairners are desperately in need of aid.

(276) The environmental lobby presents the term 'sustainable development' as an important new contribution to the choice of policies. *In particular*, it claims new insight into the weight that should be attached to the environmental impact of any economic activity and the interests of future generations. Unfortunately it is difficult to find a clear statement

of what exactly the concept means. *For example*, would some depletion of the stock of one or more particular components of the world's total stock of resources be compatible with 'sustainable development'?

ACs can simply introduce new information, such as *also* and *and* in (274). Or they can signal that the next piece of text will restate what has just been said in a different way, like *in other words* in (275). In (276), the ACs *in particular* and *for example* indicate that what follows is one instance of what has gone before.

Opposition connectives

The words *but*, *nevertheless* and *in spite of* in examples (271–3) were all OCs. Here are some more examples:

(277) Of the economists considered in Section II above, the one who was interested in the relation of firms to markets was Marshall. Marshall, *however*, chose to go in a different direction. His contemporaries, *on the other hand*, *though* they developed the theory of competitive equilibrium, were interested in issues other than that of the relationship of the firm to the industry.

(278) What on earth do I stay in this relationship for? He treats me as if I don't exist. He drinks, has relationships with other women, and generally treats me as a charlady. And *yet*, I love the so-and-so.

(279) Questions to the PM yesterday were a dismal affair. James Cran (Con, Beverley) wanted tourists and 'almost' (he said) 'everybody else who comes to the UK' to realise that using British airports was 'almost' (he said) 'as safe as anywhere in the world'. . . . This was the dreary scene that it had been Mr Kinnock's hope to enliven with a spirited question on interest rates. *At least*, it was supposed to be spirited.

OCs indicate that what follows is in some sense opposed to, or contrasted with, what has come before. The OC *at least* in (279) warns the reader that what follows will correct what has just been said. We would expect to find OCs used in conjunction with the 'opposites' that we looked at in Chapter 4: if you look back you will see, for instance, that examples (63), (65), (67) and (80) contain the OCs *while*, *whereas*, *but* and *though*.

Cause connectives

CCs indicate that two chunks of text are related as cause and effect. The most common CC is *because*, illustrated in examples (35), (97) and (223). Another is *therefore*, illustrated here:

(280) Property analysts have failed to see that south-east Wales has changed in ten years from a 'smokestack

region' to being one of the most advanced economies in the UK. Unlike many parts of south-east England, south-east Wales has no large surplus of office space. An increased demand could *therefore* lead to stock shortages and an increase in rental values.

Other CCs are *as a result* (71), *hence* and *for the same reason* in (244), and *with a view to* in (196).

Time connectives

TCs can indicate sequence, as we saw with *then* in (270). They can also indicate that two events are simultaneous, as with *just then* in (174). Expressions such as *at first* and *finally* (cf. example 245) are also TCs, as is *before* in this example:

> (281) Recently, interest in local government autonomy has revived in some countries. But the question of how long this will last, *before* central control re-emerges on the scene, has to be raised.

In the last chapter we distinguished between text reference and situation reference. Some connectives can also be used in these two different ways. Compare how the TC *finally* is used in these two examples:

> (282) Placed in the middle of a field of alfalfa, foraging bees will fly tremendous distances to find alternative sources of food. Modern agricultural practices and the finite flight range of honey bees, however, often bring bees to a grim choice between foraging on alfalfa or starving. In the face of potential starvation, honey bees finally begin foraging on alfalfa, but they learn to avoid being hurt.

> (283) Where local government exists, field administrators can play very important supervisory and supportive roles. . . . These roles can be especially important when local government is in its infancy. Field officers can also provide protection for the public by commenting on proposals which may have adverse effects locally. . . . Finally, the presence of senior officials in the field may in itself be developmental because it may result in facilities being provided which otherwise would not have been.

In (282) *finally* refers to the sequence of events described in the text. In (283), *finally* refers to the development of the text rather than to a sequence of events outside the text.

Notice also that the same word or phrase can often function as two different types of connective. Compare the two instances of *since* in these examples:

(284) Citizens-band (CB) radio and ham-operated stations are also on the increase. In little over a year since the British government gave its approval to CB, the Home Office has been inundated with six to eight thousand complaints of interference each month.

(285) David got out of bed, discharged himself and, since friends had taken his clothes, left the hospital clad in his pyjamas and dressing-gown. We got a taxi home.

In (284), *since* means 'since the time when' and is a TC; in (285) it means 'because' and is a CC. We'll see some more examples like this in the following exercises.

✐ **EXERCISES**

1. The underlined expressions in the following examples are all connectives. Say what type of connective each is:

A. Success with a new product is generating excitement about one of Japan's staple foodstuffs, the soyabean. Japanese people consume the nutritious legume mainly as tofu (bean curd), or miso, a thick brown salty paste used for flavouring. Several years ago, miso came under fire from researchers who claimed that it caused high blood pressure, *then* Japan's number one killer. Predictably, sales slumped *as a result*. *Now* to the miso producers' rescue has come tonyu – soya-milk. *In fact*, soyamilk is not new. The Chinese have drunk it hot, for more than 2000 years. (286)

> **Model Answer:**
>
> *then*: TC
> *as a result*: CC
> *now*: TC
> *in fact*: OC

B. I never knock another man's beliefs, and *in turn* I expect to be respected for mine. *Stated very simply*, I face reality and admit that *not only* isn't there anyone at home upstairs – there isn't *even* any upstairs. I have one life *and* intend to make the most of it. *Therefore* it follows naturally that I cannot deprive another person of their turn at existence. Only the very self-assured political and religious zealots kill people *in order to* save them. Live and let live, I say. Help the good guys *and* kick out the bad. (287)

C. At independence, Kenya inherited an elaborate framework of 'para-statals' (*that is*, publicly-owned enterprises) *especially* in the agricultural sector. *In view of its aims of* promoting development, decolonising the country, increasing citizen participation in the economy and ensuring more public control of the economy, the Government established more para-statals. *As a result*, para-statals are *now* to be found in all sectors of the economy – *for example*, in agriculture, commerce, industry, tourism, housing, construction, insurance, banking, basic services, etc. (288)

D. Map information is conveyed by means of symbols, words and colour or shading. . . . Information on maps is conveyed also by the patterns of lines, shading and symbols *and* this is the point at which recognition and relationships can become confused. *Thus*, a town will be recognised by the name lettering, the combination of housing and road symbols, etc. *Nevertheless*, the primary activity will be the recognition and identification of the main features of the town. *Similarly*, other geographical features may be recognised by simple relative patterns: *for example*, contour lines and water lines may give information about drainage patterns, river basins and watersheds. (289)

E. They were discussing Walter Sisulu's visit to London in 1953 *when* David had been delegated to escort Walter to meetings. Everyone wanted to know about Mr Sisulu *as* he had been in the South African struggle for fifteen years. He'd been repeatedly arrested and jailed. He was charged under the Suppression of Communism Act, David said, in 1952, after the Defiance Campaign Against Unjust Laws – *when* I had sat waiting to be arrested in Joubert Park on my own – *then* banned and confined to the magisterial district of Johannesburg. *Nevertheless*, he had been on the national action committee which had formed the Congress of Democrats in 1953. '*In spite of* all the restrictions on him, Walter Sisulu is at the very heart of the liberation movement in South Africa,' David said. (290)

2. Pick out and classify the connectives in these examples:

A. 'We must not underestimate the dangers of solvent abuse. This is not a problem that has gone away. In fact, it is getting worse. The figures are there, after all, for everyone to see: 145 deaths in 1990 was the highest ever. That's two or three children every week, and the terrible thing is it can happen the first time.' (291)

B. Merocaine is a throat lozenge with proven power. The reason for its proven effectiveness is that Merocaine contains two carefully selected ingredients that provide powerful and rapid relief when a severe sore throat strikes. (292)

C. It was a happy end to a pleasant evening. I hummed to myself as I did an easy breaststroke through the darkness. I had brought joy to this dull planet, at least for a few brief moments. The police had reluctantly indulged in a bit of exercise. Now they could relax and fill out the endless reports so dear to a copper's heart. The news reporters would have something interesting to write about – for a change – and the populace in turn would be fascinated by the exciting events of the evening. I really should be treated as a benefactor of mankind – not a criminal. But there is no justice. (293)

D. Living organisms constantly use energy to synthesise the compounds of which they are made. They also use energy to perform osmotic, mechanical and electrical work. ... Energy is made available when energy-rich substances are oxidised in living cells during respiration. Thus photosynthesis and respiration bring about the conversion of sunlight into energy. ... In this context it is useful to know about a substance called adenosine 5'-triphosphate (ATP), which was first isolated by Lohmann from muscle extracts in 1929. Ten years later Lipmann suggested that ATP transfers energy from energy-rich substrates to energy-requiring processes in living cells. (294)

E. The Bishop of Lincoln, the Right Revd Robert Hardy, was heartened last year when the general chapter passed a motion expressing no confidence that the dean and chapter would reconcile their differences and called on the canons to consider their positions. On Monday night, however, the position of the general chapter appeared to swing in favour of the canons. On a motion calling on the canons to resign and another calling on Canon Davis to hand over as treasurer, eighteen canons voted against, eight abstained, and only seven voted in favour. Two reasons were later suggested for the change of mind. Some reported a feeling that it is simply not done to pass judgement on fellow clergy. More important was a memo from the dean, written in November, in which he demanded the resignation of Canons Davis, Rutter and Nurser. Dr Jackson's advice to Canon Rutter was: 'You are a sick man and you are not capable of carrying out the duties of precentor and the cathedral is suffering as a result.' The memo, leaked to the magazine *Private Eye* last week, is thought by many in the general chapter to be tactless and confrontational. (295)

---

3. One connective which can be used in more than one way is *anyway*. Look at these examples:

(296) One thing I can always talk to my dad about is food. He likes to describe to me, in detail, the restaurant meals he has had recently. His latest thing is cheese shops: he must drive the shopkeepers crazy by insisting on trying out every variety. He adores European cheeses – French and Swiss ones, anyway – and has just discovered some interesting Italian kinds in the local cheese emporium.

(297) Sir Keith made plain his dislike of the financial mechanisms with which governments in the West habitually support industrial companies. 'It [the UK Government] could only provide substantial extra resources to industry either by cutting public spending elsewhere or by raising taxes or by increased borrowing. ... The damage done to industry by any of these three methods would probably be more than the good done to it by the direct help and anyway I am not clear on the sort of direct help that might be intended.'

(298) Dear Wendy,
I didn't forget – but such is the state of organisation around here that your card is getting posted not one but five days late. I'm sorry – but getting to the PO for a stamp just took a bit of planning this year!
Happy birthday anyway twin! And thanks very much for sending me a card – on time too!

In (296), *anyway* means 'at least'; in (297) it means 'besides' or 'in any case', and in (298) it means something like 'this is a new topic'.

✎ Decide how *anyway* is used in these extracts:

(A) The news from English Heritage yesterday that over 900 listed historic buildings in London are at risk of serious decay is a poor comment on conservation legislation. If listing, conservation areas and grants cannot protect buildings worth keeping in a wealthy capital, what hope is there for the rest of the country? The solution is not merely more of the same, including money. The time has come for a shift in government policy. The philistine might retort that there are too many buildings being saved anyway, and that the most dilapidated should be written off. Given the destruction already wrought by poor planning on London, the case for loosening controls is weak. (299)

(B) It seems hardly conceivable now that, after England had lost the last Test Match at Sydney in 1986–7, with only seven balls left, I said to the England captain, Mike Gatting, that the result was to be welcomed as a good one for cricket. Having already lost the Ashes, and practically everything else for the previous two years, Australia were in urgent need of all the encouragement they could get. Gatting, of course, replied, 'You may think so, Wooders, but I most certainly don't,' and at this distance his reply makes a lot more sense than my hypothesis. It is, anyway, an international sportsman's duty to want to win and to win and to win again. (300)

(C) The best advice to beginners is to look around, try out a lot of bikes, and see which one you feel most comfortable with. Buy the best bike you can afford – not a cheap old wreck, anyway – and spend some time and a little money on maintaining it in good working order and replacing parts that wear out. Pay particular attention to the brakes, tyres, chainset, gears and pedals, and use WD 40 (not oil) every week or so. (301)

(D) I just went out to work for a company called 'Schools Abroad', a travel company that dealt specifically with schools and colleges, and I worked for them as a ski technician and that allowed me to work for about two hours a week and I'd ski eight hours a day seven days a week, you see. After about a month I was getting pretty good, 'cos I was a good skier anyway but after spending about two months out on the snow I was getting really hot, so everybody started to hear about this Englishman who was getting on really well at the skiing and getting really fast and things. Then this local guy came to me – he was the super-hot skier of the whole country – and he came up to me and offered me a race. (302)

4. Here are some examples of other connectives which can be used in more than one way. For each group of examples, try to paraphrase the connective to bring out the different uses.

In fact (Compare also example 286):

(A) Most of us have been taught to see the Davy lamp as a scientific advance in that it saved the lives of miners because it would burn without causing explosions in a methane-rich atmosphere. In fact, Albany and Schwartz tell us, the Davy lamp enabled the managers of the mines to extend operations into seams with dangerous atmospheres, so when accidents did occur, the chances of being killed were far higher. (303)

(B) A good example of a really large-scale anarchist revolution − in fact the best example to my knowledge − is the Spanish revolution in 1936, in which over most of Republican Spain there was a quite inspiring anarchist revolution that involved both industry and agriculture over substantial areas . . . [it] was, by both human measures and indeed anyone's economic measures, quite successful. That is, production continued effectively; workers in farms and factories proved quite capable of managing their affairs without coercion from above. (304)

(C) The case of the diabetic who took insulin for fifty-two years, only to turn out not to need it at all, is bemusing doctors. For most of his life, doctors had assumed that the man was incapable of making his own insulin in the cells of his pancreas. In fact he had been churning it out all along. To compensate for the huge doses injected into his body every day, his immune system had evolved to recognise the alien insulin and to deactivate it. (305)

Actually:

(D) Another class of transformations are those that alter size, but not shape. . . . A triangle will be transformed into a curvilinear (actually, circular) triangle, whose curved sides will not possess the relative proportions of the original triangle, but the angles measured at the corners will not be altered. (306)

(E) Now we come to the heart of the matter. For how do we decide which meaning the linguist has in his mind? The obvious suggestion is that we should ask him. (Actually, we have assumed that our linguist does not speak the language well enough to do this. Even if he can, though, the problem remains the same.) (307)

(F) With the *Sainsbury Choir of the Year* currently showing on BBC2, Lord Sainsbury is well aware of the benefits to be gained from this kind of 'own-label' sponsorship, giving the company a product identification not unlike its own brands of soap powder and baked beans. 'It's very good for the company in the sense that there are choirs from all over the land and in the choral movement everyone's heard of the *Sainsbury Choir of the Year* award.' And, he adds, getting to the real point of it all, 'it actually has helped raise choral standards.' (308)

Now:

(G) Figures for July show house prices in the UK to be virtually unchanged from a month ago, rising by just 0.1 per cent, the Halifax reports. Over the past three months national house prices have risen by just 1.8 per cent with the overall pattern remaining similar to that reported last month. House prices in the South are now 5 to 10 per cent below their peak of late last year, which reflects the fact that sellers are accepting more realistic prices for their properties. (309)

(H) Interviewing politicians is always entertaining because they always have something to say and they come in determined to say it. Now that seems to me the way the game goes. The job of the interviewer is to make sure first of all that they say what they intended to say. And then if what they've said appears to be in conflict with the known evidence, you then say, well wait a minute, how do you reconcile what you've just said with what we all know? (310)

(I) Video is just another aid at your disposal. Even if you are new to it, you probably already have a range of ideas for language work which could perfectly well apply to video.

We turn now from materials with a focus on language to materials you choose because of the topic they present. (311)

---

5. In the following texts the connectives have been removed. Try to work out what the connectives might be. The missing connectives are indicated by stars, each star representing exactly one word; [**] means one connective consisting of two words, while [*] [*] means two one-word connectives next to each other. Try to think of several possible connectives in each case.

(A) [**] most UK playgroups and nurseries are entirely female preserves, and the man who regularly puts in as many hours with his child as he does at his work is rare. * a draft proposal for a European Commission recommendation on childcare suggests this could change. The proposal, published next month, aims to promote equal treatment of the sexes in the labour market. It * calls for action to encourage men as child carers, * for more public funding for pre-school education. (312)

Model Answer:

At present most UK playgroups and nurseries are entirely female preserves, and the man who regularly puts in as many hours with his child as he does at his work is rare. *But* a draft proposal for a European Commission recommendation on childcare suggests this could change. The proposal, published next month, aims to promote equal treatment of the sexes in the labour market. It *therefore* calls for action to encourage men as childcarers, *and* for more public funding for pre-school education.

(B) * she met Martin he'd never seen her perform. * Bette wasn't in the least bothered, * he made her laugh, which was more important to her. The couple married in 1984, and Bette's happiness was made complete in 1986 when Sophie was born. Bette was 40 years old *, * she planned two more children. [*] [**] more children have eluded her. * Bette does not dwell on the fact, * concentrates * on counting her blessings. (313)

(C) * you have a number of files and directories on a disk, it is not always easy to tell which disk you are working with, * if it could be any one of a number that you haven't used for some time. You can make things much simpler by giving each of your disks a disk label – [**], an individual name of up to eleven characters. This name is always displayed when you use the DIR command to list any directory on the disk, * one's way down the directory tree – * you have a very easy way to tell which disk it is. (314)

(D) Whether Mrs Honour really deserved that suspicion of which her mistress gave her a hint, is a matter which we cannot indulge our reader's curiosity by resolving. We will * make him amends, in disclosing what passed in the mind of Sophia.

The reader will be pleased to recollect that a secret affection for Mr Jones had insensibly stolen into the bosom of this young lady. . . . When she first began to perceive its symptoms, the sensations were so sweet and pleasing, that she had not resolution enough to check or repel them; and * she went on cherishing a passion of which she never once considered the consequences.

This incident relating to Molly first opened her eyes. She * first perceived the weakness of which she had been guilty; [*] [*] it caused the utmost perturbation in her mind, * it had the effect of other nauseous physic, and for the time expelled her distemper. Its operation was * most wonderfully quick. (315)

(E) The first goal of colonialism was wealth – for the colonial states and for individual settlers. * individual mine claims quickly became consolidated under a few 'randlords', large capital investments were necessary to develop technology to dig * deeper; *, until the late 1960s, the price of gold was fixed. [**], the price of diamonds was systematically controlled by setting up a monopoly of marketing. Planned scarcity was (and is) the key to the profitability of diamonds. For most of the minerals, *, profits depended on keeping costs low and the major, and * only, input factor which could be kept low cost was labour. (316)

(F) Talk about innate structures of whichever kind leads people to the conclusion, which many of them find unwelcome, that there could be, [**] probably will be, differences in innate capacity. * it is a very interesting question why people should find that bothersome. . . . Nobody finds it bothersome that if your parents are tall * you are likely to be tall. . . . * why should it be difficult to accept that if there is something in your genes that makes you a good violinist you are different from someone who does not have that in his genes. Generally it is liberal progressive types who find this unpleasant but I think that they are * only revealing their own deep commitment to inegalitarian ideologies. [**], the reason why many decent, honest people find it unpleasant to imagine that there might be differences in mental capacity that are biologically determined is that they have a residual belief that the way people ought to be treated or what they deserve, somehow reflects some kind of intrinsic merit. (317)

(G) You can cash your girocheque at only one particular post office, which you choose yourself. The post office may, *, ask you for proof of identity.

If you cannot get to the post office you can ask someone to cash the cheque for you. Follow the instructions on the cheque. You must sign it, and the person who cashes it must * show proof of your identity. You can * pay the cheque into your bank or building society account, if you have one. (318)

(H) I wonder if anyone has ever chosen a dictionary as the one book they would like to take with them to a desert island. It may seem a rather silly idea * there would be no other books or people around to provide the words that you would need to look up. * anyone who owns a dictionary probably knows already how tempting it is to browse around in one. You go to look up one word and find that others on the same or the opposite page catch your eye. A definition that solves one question raises another which sends you off to the other end of the book. * you are searching, you remember half a dozen other words that you meant to look up [***] but forgot to. [***] you spend at least twice as long on the task as you intended, * you don't begrudge yourself the time * looking around the book has been not only informative but fun. Dictionaries, [**], exercise a powerful fascination over anyone who is the least bit interested in words. [****] they are an essential tool for the person who wants to use words to good purpose. (319)

PART III
BEYOND COHESION

LARGER PATTERNS

10

Texts are sometimes coherent because the information in them is structured in a particular way. In analysing this kind of structure we cannot look at texts in isolation, but only in conjunction with the knowledge and expectations of language users.

So far we have looked at relationships between individual words and sentences in texts. Many texts are also organised into larger patterns which, as writers or readers, we may not be consciously aware of, but which we none the less use to help us find our way round the information in a text. One such pattern is BACKGROUND – PROBLEM – SOLUTION – EVALUATION (BPSE). The four parts of this pattern can be seen as answers to four questions, listed here along with some of the more detailed questions they subsume:

Background
Problem
Solution
Evaluation

1   What is the BACKGROUND? (What time, place, people, etc. are going to be involved in this text? What do we need to know to understand the next part, the 'problem'?)

Background

2   What is the PROBLEM that arises out of this situation? (What is this text principally about? What need, dilemma, puzzle, obstacle or lack does this text address?)

Problem

3   What is the SOLUTION to the problem? (How are or were the need met, the dilemma resolved, the puzzle solved, the obstacle overcome, or the lack remedied?)

Solution

4   How should this solution be EVALUATED? (How good is it at solving the problem? If there is more than one solution, which is best?)

Evaluated

The text given here shows the BPSE structure quite clearly (the paragraphs are numbered for convenience):

(320)   <1> It's a quiet life for Danny these days. He's in

regular work and spends most of his sparetime with his new baby. The highlight at weekends is a football game with his new friends. It took a while to find enough of them for a team. What he likes most about them is that they have no idea who he is.

<2> Last year Danny (not his real name) gave evidence in a murder trial and became part of a huge security operation by police to protect the key witnesses from intimidation.

<3> The threat to Danny's life was clear from the moment he was called out of a family celebration to talk to two friends in the car park. They told him that if he appeared as a witness he could expect the worst. . . .

<4> 'It went through my mind to do a runner. But I'd given my statement, I decided they were going to be looking for me anyway because of what I've seen, so I stuck by what I'd said.'

<5> The police increased Danny's protection as the trial date approached. He was offered an armed escort twenty-four hours a day, but settled for two unarmed plainclothes officers. The three of them spent weeks on the move, staying at small guest houses around the area, passing their days at bowling alleys and police station snooker tables, until Danny was whisked into court to give evidence.

<6> When the jury returned a verdict of not guilty the police were crestfallen. Danny, of course, felt more vulnerable than ever. He knows that one of his previous secret addresses was inadvertently registered on the DSS computer. His only security rests on the hope that the secret of his new address is kept tight. It's a dark irony, he observes, that the only people who have lost their liberty in this murder case are those, like him, who stood up to tell the truth.

The *background* is that Danny lives an almost, but not quite, normal life (first paragraph). The *problem* is that he is frightened because he has to hide his identity after witnessing a murder (second, third and fourth paragraphs). The *solution* was police protection until the trial (fifth paragraph and the first sentence of sixth paragraph). The *evaluation* of the solution is mainly negative: Danny still feels 'vulnerable', and there is the 'dark irony' mentioned in the last sentence (the rest of sixth paragraph).

Here is a different kind of text which also displays the BPSE pattern (sentences numbered for convenience):

(321) <1> In hiding with a cold sore? <2> Now, when a cold sore appears you don't have to disappear.

<3> Treat it with Lypsyl Cold Sore Gel the minute you feel that tell-tale tingle. <4> Lypsyl contains three active ingredients: an anaesthetic to relieve pain, an astringent to dry the cold sore and an anti-septic to fight infection. <5> What's more, unlike many other treatments Lypsyl Cold Sore Gel is clear, colourless and completely invisible. <6> Which means you don't have to be.

The first sentence gives the *background* (having a cold sore) and the *problem* (hiding because of it) simultaneously. The second and third sentences give a *solution* to the problem (Lypsyl Cold Sore Gel). The fourth sentence gives more details of the solution and begins to *evaluate* it. The fifth and sixth sentences continue the evaluation, which is naturally a positive one, this being an advertisement. Different parts of the BPSE pattern may thus be indicated at the same time.

Parts of the BPSE pattern may not be spelled out in a text if they are obvious from the context, or if the reader can be assumed to know what they are already. An advertisement for trousers does not need to specify that the *background* is that you have two legs and that the *problem* is that you want a garment to cover them. The advertisement can simply give a description of the trousers (*solution*) and of their many good points (*evaluation*), assuming that only readers who have the implicit problem are likely to respond. Similarly, an article in a medical journal about a particular disease does not need to state that the problem addressed is either under-standing the causes of the disease or testing a new cure: the text can assume that its readers know this in advance.

The order of the parts of a BPSE pattern can vary. Many news-paper stories lead with an outline of the *solution* to get the reader's attention. They then indicate the *problem*, more details of the *solution*, the *background*, and finally one or more *evaluations*, which may be comments by people concerned. Here is a concocted example (paragraphs numbered for convenience):

(322) PM IN CALL FOR MORE INEQUALITY

<1> The Prime Minister said today that the poor must expect to get poorer, and the rich richer. Only in this way could Britain get inflation under control.

<2> The PM said that the bottom strata of society must stop pricing themselves out of jobs and should blame themselves for being poor. The minority of speculators and entrepreneurs at the top, on the other hand, created wealth through hard work and should be encouraged to earn more.

<3> Speaking at the opening of the Reigate Rehabilitation Centre for Greedy Executives, the Prime Minister spoke against a background of high

unemployment and increasing social discontent. The government's standing in the opinion polls is at an all time low, and senior party officials have urged the Prime Minister to 'think again'.

<4> City reaction was positive, with most major shares making gains. The Leader of the Opposition described the Prime Minister's remarks as 'badly timed' and 'unfair'.

The headline and the opening sentence outline the *solution*, while the next sentence gives the *problem*. The second paragraph gives more details of the *solution*, while the third paragraph sets out the *background*. The last paragraph provides two *evaluations* of the proposed solution.

The cohesive devices that we looked at in earlier chapters help us to distinguish new information from old information in a text. A series of sentences without cohesive devices can give the impression of conveying completely new information in each sentence, unrelated to old information from previous sentences. Often, however, we can draw on our background knowledge or clues from the context so that we can organise the information without the help of cohesive devices.

The BPSE pattern goes beyond this: assuming that we are able to distinguish between new and old information (either with the help of cohesive devices or in other ways), the BPSE pattern is a way of indicating how the information is *relevant*, or what the point of saying it is. The key part of the pattern is probably the *problem*: once we know which part of the text sets out the problem, the relevance of the other parts of the text becomes easier to figure out.

Cohesive devices thus help to make a text coherent, but are not necessary or sufficient to create coherence on their own. A structure such as the BPSE pattern is more crucial in creating coherence. Example (18) in Chapter 1 had plenty of cohesive devices (more accurately, plenty of instances of one cohesive device, word repetition) but was incoherent: it lacked the BPSE pattern (or any other pattern). Compare this example, which has almost no cohesive devices but does have a clear BPSE pattern:

(323) 6.15 p.m. Called round about the project. Where were you? I'll try to ring tomorrow. A few quick decisions should be enough. Best wishes – Ruby.

Cohesive devices are part of the resources of a language. The BPSE pattern, in contrast, involves interaction between language and the knowledge, beliefs and expectations of language users. The exact nature of this interaction is a central issue in advanced work in text and discourse analysis.

1. Analyse these texts in terms of the BPSE pattern, explaining whether they incorporate the whole pattern or just part of it.

 A. A decade or so ago, Professor James Coleman and his colleagues encountered a surprising research finding in their investigation of how medical doctors decided to adopt a new antibiotic drug. Each of the doctors knew about the extensive scientific evaluations of the antibiotic drug by university medical schools and pharmaceutical firms. But this information did not convince the doctors to begin prescribing the new drug for their patients.

 The typical doctor did not adopt the new drug until a colleague who had previously adopted it relayed his subjective evaluations of it. When the colleague said, 'Look, Doctor, I have used this new drug with my patients, and it works,' the doctor was likely to try it. This peer influence was especially influential if the colleague was socially similar, such as by having graduated from the same medical school, having a similar medical practice, and being of about the same age. (324)

Model Answer:

B – surprising research finding
P – why doctors adopted drug
S – evaluations by universities and firms
E – did not convince doctors
S – peer recommendation
E – especially influential if . . .

 B. DESCRIBING SPEECH SOUNDS

 The plural suffix in *cats* is an 's-sound', whereas in *bushes* it consists of a vowel plus a 'z-sound'. Moreover, the plural suffix is pronounced as a single z-sound (that is, without a preceding vowel) in words such as *dogs*. . . .

 The 's-sound' is produced by air flowing from the lungs and passing through a narrow passage between the tongue tip and the roof of the mouth. The same hissing sound characterizes the 'z' variant of the plural suffix (as in *dogs*), but in this case the sound is perceived as having more of a buzz. There is, in fact, an additional noise source in the throat that accompanies the production of the z. But expressions such as 'noise source in the throat' are not very precise, and in order to understand the nature of speech sounds, we need a more detailed examination of the anatomical structures involved in speech. (325)

C. DOCTOR BOOX AND THE SORE GIRAFFE

One morning, rather late, Doctor Boox was lying in bed with a few dogs and hamsters when the telephone rang.

'Boox here,' said Boox. 'What do you want?'

'Schmitt itty Shoo Shah,' said the telephone.

'Can't hear a word you're saying,' said Boox. This was because he had his stethoscope stuck in his ears. He always kept it there to be on the safe side. He took it off and gave it to a dog to hold.

'This is the zoo,' said the telephone. 'We've got a sore giraffe here.'

'Where is it sore?' said Boox.

'In the neck,' said the man on the telephone.

'Oh dear,' said Boox, 'I was afraid of that.'

'Well, can you help?'

'Oh, I'll have a go,' said Boox. He put the phone down.

'Right lads,' said Boox to the dogs. 'We're off to the zoo.'

'Row! Row! Row!' shouted the dogs.

[On the way Boox gets stuck up a lamppost and is rescued by the fire brigade.]

When they got to the zoo they drove straight up to the giraffe, who was very sore indeed now and rather cross. But Boox got out his bottle of liniment (on the label it said *Doctor Boox's double strength neck rub*) and rubbed the giraffe's neck with it. After a bit the giraffe said:

'Ahhhhh.'

'He's better now,' said Boox.

'Thank you very much,' said the Zoo man.

'Good old Boox,' said the firemen. (326)

D. Since 1972, the Philippines' national debt has risen from $2.7 billion to $29 billion. Much of this is the result of secret and often fraudulent deals by the dictator Ferdinand Marcos. The World Bank and the International Monetary Fund quietly approved of Marcos and worked to keep him in power. . . .

As in its other client states, the World Bank set out to undermine an economy that had the capacity to feed the population. The instrument was a strategy called 'export-led industrialisation', which was ideologically based and of minimal economic worth. . . . The current demands of the IMF are for further reductions in public spending, a freeze on wages and new taxes. . . . In 1989 the Department of Health said that IMF demands would mean that 399,000 children would be denied milk and vitamins, and 103,000 tuberculosis sufferers medical treatment. The implication is clear: tens of thousands of children will die 'silently' and unnecessarily.

Elizabeth, aged 3, and Lito, aged 2, were two of these children. Eddie took Elizabeth to the local hospital when her diarrhoea 'would not stop'. The hospital said they would take the child, but Eddie would have to buy the medicines in the market. The cheapest he could find cost forty pesos. So he scavenged for a day and got it. But Elizabeth was now seriously ill; and so, too, was Lito whose stomach had distended in a matter of days. Teresita told me how she watched, horrified, as worms emerged from the mouth of her skeletal child. On the day they buried Elizabeth, in a cemetery occupied mostly by the unmarked graves of children, Lito died too. (327)

E. THE LAST DAYS OF *CHEZ NOUS*

The new film by Gillian Armstrong, director of *My Brilliant Career* and *High Tide*, is an intimate urban drama about the uncertainties of love, spanning a single hot summer in Sydney. *Chez Nous* is a rambling Victorian terrace inhabited by Beth (Lisa Harrow), who enjoys hard earned success as a writer, her French husband (Bruno Ganz) and teenage daughter. It is at once a refuge and a war zone – a retreat from the outside world and the site of the film's cruellest betrayals. Dominated by Beth, tensions in the eccentric household are held in check by domestic rituals and evasions. But it proves to be a delicate balance, upset by the return of Beth's admiring, dependent and selfish younger sister (Kerry Fox). It is the strangely enmeshed lives of these two women, one old enough to be the younger one's mother, that provides the film's emotional core. (328)

---

2. When we look for a pattern in a text, we are often helped by words which indicate parts of the pattern. These words include, of course, the four we have used for the parts of the BPSE pattern:

(329) Tom King, the defence secretary, yesterday gave a warning to British and American businessmen and

the public against giving in to terrorism. He said that, as Northern Ireland secretary, he had learnt a little of the way that terrorists operated. They committed one act and hoped through propaganda to spread that terror ever more widely so that millions of people would change their behaviour and concede to the terrorist threat. One of the wonderful things about Northern Ireland had been the way ordinary people had carried on living normal lives. It was against that *background* that he was worried about the reaction to the threat of world terrorism today.

(330) Engineers have long wrestled with the *problems* of safeguarding equipment against radio-frequency interference (RFI). One *solution* is simply to shield the device, by enclosing it in a metal or plastic box of low impedance. Unfortunately, unless the device is skilfully earthed the shielding often has little effect. . . . In *evaluating* alternative strategies, cost, ease of use, effectiveness and transportability are crucial considerations.

Problem

Other words can be used to highlight the PROBLEM:

(331) *Search* is a journal of science in Australia and New Zealand, its cover pronounces. I had not seen it before taking a look at the February/March issue. *One depressing surprise, though*, was afforded me by a report on neighbourhood shopping centres. Many of us have the idea of Australians, above all, being people who call a spade a spade. *But* town planning and sociology in Australia evidently produce the same junk words as they do elsewhere. 'There was no change in the number of establishments devoted to the sale of comparison goods', for example. Bought any comparison goods lately?

(332) Hand puppets made to look like mature Californian condors are being used by biologists at the San Diego wild animal park to nurse the first two Californian condor chicks born in captivity through the early weeks of life. Their diet consists of chopped two-day old mice, and vulture's vomit. The turkey and black vultures at the park are well fed and then scared into bringing up their food to supply the chicks. The chicks have taken Indian names after regions of their natural habitat. Sisquoc was born on 30 March and has more than doubled his weight of 201.9 grams. Tecuya is smaller, 165.9 grams at birth on 5 April, and is causing some *concern*.

(333) The Foreign Office yesterday summoned the Iraqi ambassador to deliver a *protest* at reports of *death* and *injury* to allied prisoners of war used as human shields. Douglas Hogg, the junior minister at the Foreign Office, told Azmi Shafiq al-Salihi that Britain demanded Iraq's full compliance with the Geneva conventions, and would hold those responsible for breaches 'personally liable'.

A variety of words can indicate SOLUTIONS: **Solutions**

(334) GATT CHIEF TO REVEAL *PLAN* FOR SAVING TALKS

Arthur Dunkel, director general of the General Agreement on Tariffs and Trade (Gatt), is to present informal *proposals* to top trade officials for reviving the Uruguay round talks on world trade.

(335) *Answering* widespread concern in the US about America's share of the burden of Operation Desert Storm, the President said: 'Only the United States of America has both the moral standing and the means to back it up. We are the only nation on earth who could assemble the forces of peace.'

(336) Roith is determined to make science and technology central to the department's policy. He has *set up* a science and technology management group within the DoI (Department of Industry) which coordinates the work of its different divisions.

✎ In the following texts, pick out the words and phrases which mark part of the BPSE pattern.

A. Cabinet hopes of keeping average poll tax bills below £400 this year suffered a serious setback last night when the first council in England to decide on its community charge approved an increase of 16 per cent. (337)

B. The attacks that extremist groups have been able to launch have not been very successful so far. One Iraqi has been killed in Manila, possibly the bomber himself, but there are no reports of injuries and only minimal damage to buildings. (338)

C. Your tribute to Derailleur, who as you reminded readers (*This Week*, 21 April, p. 135) 'invented his [bicycle gear] system in the 1920s' was as welcome as it was belated. But Derailleur is only one of the many forgotten pioneers of road transport. Some of course achieved recognition in other fields. But they were not the greatest: the mechanical acoustic early warning device of Alexander Graham Bell (his first essay in telecommunications) is rarely heard nowadays. Likewise, Jean Monod's inertial approach, for all its Gallic elegance, has failed to displace the old non-inertial guidance system of Handel and Barr – now quite forgotten. Monod, by his collaboration with Coque, at least left a name in the automotive industry, but who today ever gives a thought to Le Chassis, without whose basic contribution to the theory of tetracyclic separation that industry would never have got off the ground? Do give us more. (339)

D. The world's intelligence agencies are, for the first time, pooling their resources to tackle the threat of terrorist attacks by supporters of President Saddam Hussein. (340)

E. The Foreign and Commonwealth Office (FCO) has neither accepted nor refused Smiley's request for permission to build himself a family-sized mansion and an airstrip on Henderson. The FCO is waiting, it says, for Ratliff to clarify his plans before it comes to a decision. Unfortunately, it is not simply the future of Henderson Island which is at stake. In return for permission to reside on Henderson, Smiley Ratliff has promised to provide the inhabitants of nearby Pitcairn Island with the use of his proposed airstrip, a launch to ferry them the ninety or so miles between Pitcairn and Henderson. (341)

F. A survey of 640 company directors in four countries suggests that a growing number of experienced managers in Europe are ready to leave the security of large companies to set up their own businesses. Sharp national differences emerged on a number of issues. Germans were likely to want to set up on their own because of frustration at missed career opportunities, while 83 per cent of those surveyed in France wanted freedom from bureaucracy. (342)

G. When the people of a country try to free themselves from the US grip, the US response ranges from diplomatic pressure and economic boycotts to subversion, political interference, assassination, terrorism, backing for military coups, or direct invasion by the most powerful military force in history. (343)

H. A colleague of mine returning from a remote part of Kenya commented on the habit among pregnant women of eating a particular sort of yellowish mud. The practice, which I gather is fairly widespread in

Africa, appears to be effective in warding off anaemia, presumably due to a high iron concentration in the mud. (344)

✎ Carry out the same procedure for examples 52, 55, 66, 68, 85, 123, 132, 133, 188, 191, 231, 254, 286, 307 and 314.

---

3. Try to find or write some coherent texts which use only parts of the BPSE structure, or which change the order of the parts around. In particular, look for examples of PS and ESPB. (The following examples are relevant: 19, 23, 46, 118, 123, 180.)

FURTHER EXERCISES

1. The cohesive devices that have appeared in this book all looked backwards: they related the current part of the text to a previous part. Some cohesive devices can look forward. For instance, Chapter 3 examined texts such as (36) where the hyponym came first, then the superordinate. Here are some examples where the order is reversed. Pick out the hyponyms and superordinates. Why do you think the reverse order works in these texts but not in the texts in Chapter 3?

A. Rocks are composed of minerals of which the most common are the iron oxides (4 per cent of rock minerals), calcite and dolomite (9 per cent), kaolinites or clay minerals (18 per cent), quartz (28 per cent) and the feldspar group (33 per cent). The most common landscape forming rocks are the sedimentary shales, sandstones, limestones and the igneous granites and basalts. (345)

B. In England, as early as 1236, street pageantry included such scenic splendours as castles, columns painted to represent marble and jasper, angels descending on wires, gigantic puppets, Noah's Ark, a great dragon spouting fire, a desert with trees and a well, God appearing in a cloud, and Lucifer going down to Hell. (346)

C. In the final year, a number of special option courses allow specialisation in areas of particular interest to the student. These normally include: Syntax, Semantics and Pragmatics; Second Language Acquisition; Discourse Analysis; Stylistics; and Experimental Phonetics. (347)

D. Human speech is produced by organs of speech.

102

These fall into three groups: the first is the lungs, and their associated muscles, the bronchial tubes and the trachea (windpipe). The second is located at the opening of the trachea into the throat: this is the larynx. The third set, the articulators, consists of the various components of the mouth described below. (348)

---

2. Reference words (see Chapter 8) can also refer forwards as well as backwards. This is called CATAPHORA, or cataphoric reference, as opposed to the more common process of ANAPHORA, which is reference back. Here is an example:

Cataphora
Anaphora

(349) The key to protection of endangered species is to ensure local people receive some economic benefit back from the animal. Some countries could achieve that through trade in skins and hides from elephants which have to be culled. To *its* credit, the World Wildlife Fund has adopted this sensible compromise.

✎ Pick out the instances of cataphora in these examples:

A. The idea that violence is something really rather, you know, what the best people do ... and the implied message that the bullets don't actually hit people and don't actually kill people permeates, and there's a tremendous amount of unreality, of course, in Dallas, and suchlike. Mind you, I will say this, that in my experience at meetings, talking to people and so on – Dallas is so unreal in British terms that I think a lot of what happens there is, as we would say, taken with a pinch of salt. (350)

B. I tried to tell them but Frans laughed.
   'Jesus! Listen to this:
   'There's this guy, you know, old van der Merwe, comes into a pub, sitting there, talking to himself, shaking his head sadly, then looking around him. His friend comes up to him.
   '"Hey Van!" he says. "Wat mekeer jou, man?"' (351)

C. Cousin Bertie went away,
   To do his bit the other day.
   With a smile on his lips and his lieutenant pips
   Upon his shoulder bright and gay.
   As the train pulled out he said,
   Remember me to all the birds,
   Then he wagged his paw and went away to war
   Shouting out these pathetic words:

'Good byee, Good byee,
Wipe the tear, baby dear, from your eyee.'

[First World War song] (352)

D. The town was quiet, too quiet. His gun in his hand,
the Marshall crept behind the deserted buildings,
waiting for the men who had sworn to kill him. Now
it was just them and him, and someone must die.
(353)

E. That old black magic has me in its spell
That old black magic that you weave so well,
Those icy fingers up and down my spine
That same old witchcraft when your eyes meet mine
. . .
In a spin, loving the spin I'm in,
Under that old black magic called love.

[1930s song] (354)

Predictive devices

3. The phenomenon of 'referring forward' introduced in the last two exercises is part of a broader class of what we shall call PREDICTIVE DEVICES: ways of creating an expectation of what will come next in a text. By creating and satisfying such expectations, predictive devices contribute to coherence.

Enumeration

One such predictive device is ENUMERATION, especially when the total is announced in advance:

(355) For each Investment Fund there are two relevant unit prices.

1. *The offer price.* Units are allocated by reference to an 'offer price' which incorporates an initial management charge of 5 per cent.

2. *The bid price.* For the purpose of determining the value of benefits or meeting administration charges the 'bid' price is used. The current difference between the 'bid' and 'offer' prices is 5 per cent of the offer prices. (Compare also examples 15 and 72.)

Another is promising to do something in the text:

(356) Chapter 2 – Representation of relief, drainage and coasts

This chapter *will consider* in particular various methods of representing the natural features of the physical topography, i.e. the relief, drainage and coastlines. The representation of distributions, point and line information other than that relating to natural features *will be considered* in Chapter 3.

(Notice that, as well as the words highlighted, the chapter title in this example is also a kind of predictive device.) Other predictive devices are defining a new term, creating the assumption that it will be used later; reporting someone else's ideas, only to challenge them; and expressions such as 'as follows':

> (357) Allometry is widely observed in nature, and has been *defined* by Stephen Jay Gould, of Harvard, as 'the study of proportion changes correlated with variation in size'. What it *means* in practice, at least in the simplest cases, is that as an animal increases in overall size, various of its organs may not keep pace. . . . Huxley *argued*, in his classic *Problems of Relative Growth*, published in 1932, that allometry was found between related species as well as within species because of a common growth mechanism; a red deer is, in a broad sense, like a roe deer that has gone on growing. . . . The formal *challenge* to Lewontin and Huxley must be based on mathematical argument but the general biological points are *as follows*. One of Lewontin's examples concerns the brain size of gorillas and chimpanzees.

✎ Pick out the predictive devices in these texts:

> A. As you have elected to teach yourself Origami, by now you will be anxious to go ahead and start work on the models in this book. First, though, there is some helpful information to be considered, and the following essential instructions should be read carefully. (358)

> B. How important is vanadium scavenging by vent-derived iron oxides to the vanadium cycle? Previous geochemical balances for vanadium assumed no vanadium uptake from sea water by hydrothermal precipitates, relating essentially all of the vanadium removal to 'authigenic subtraction' in the upper water column. We believe, however, that available data on global venting provide sufficient information to show that scavenging of vanadium by hydrothermal iron oxides is an important 'authigenic' removal mechanism that needs to be factored into the global vanadium cycle. (359)

> C. In the closing decades of the nineteenth century discussion of the transfer mechanism was stimulated by a number of works analysing the terms of trade between England and India. Many of these writings relied on Mill's earlier ideas. Bastable claimed that Mill had omitted to allow for the effect of the transfer on

incomes. Bastable's theory was taken up a few years later by Nicholson (1897), who improved on it in several ways. 'Assume,' he said, 'that, in the first place, actual money is taken from the pockets of the people. We may suppose that in consequence there will be partly a lessened demand for imports and partly an excess of home commodities available for export. At the same time the receiving country – when the money is sent to it – will have so much more to spend and can take more imports and also consume things formerly exported.' (360)

D. Human rights are a fundamental issue which will be discussed at the Commonwealth Heads of Government Meeting which starts tomorrow, but it would be unfortunate if donors tied the giving of aid to the development of human rights, President Mugabe said yesterday.

Asked why he advocated sanctions against South Africa if he did not like conditions being set by donors, he said the South African situation was different in that it was South Africans who were pressing for sanctions. Zimbabwe and other Commonwealth countries were simply supporting the efforts of the oppressed people in that country. (361)

E. Boredom and drabness, Victor said, were the things he dreaded most.

Dolores tried to think what she dreaded most. Not death, not pain, bad as those were, because there was no point in dreading them, they were inevitable. Not natural catastrophe, bad as it was, because there was no point in dreading it since it was unpredictable. She knew what she dreaded most: the complete take-over of the world by a mentality she privately called Nazi. No relation to any political party in any political party in any country; found everywhere, indigenous on planet Earth. And gaining every day. (362)

✎ Try to predict what comes next after some of the extracts in this book. Say what it is in the extract that 'predicts' what is likely to come next.

_____

4. In this exercise you are given two texts which have fewer cohesive devices than normal. Text A is from a children's book. Text B was written by an adult whose first language is not English. Each text is also 'simple' in other ways, which are not relevant here (short sentences, limited vocabulary, etc.). For each text say which cohesive devices are used and which are not. Then think about these questions:

✎ *For text A*: Why do you think certain cohesive devices are used but not others? If this text was rewritten with more cohesive devices, would it help or hinder a child who is learning to read?

✎ *For text B*: Do you think the writer of this text can recognise other cohesive devices in texts that she/he reads, but does not use them in her/his own writing – or is it more likely that she/he cannot handle these devices at all? Would it be helpful if learners of English as a second language were explicitly taught about cohesive devices?

A. Peter is at home.
    He wants to go and play in the meadow, but the gate is closed.
    A bird is up in the tree in the meadow. The bird sings to Peter. Come into the meadow.
    Yes, says Peter. Here I come.
    He opens the gate and goes into the meadow.
    Peter plays in the meadow.
    The bird sings up in the tree.
    A duck comes into the meadow.
    She goes for a swim.
    The bird flies down from the tree.
    The bird says to the duck, You are a silly bird. You can't fly. See, I can fly.
    The duck says to the bird, You are a silly bird. You can't swim. See, I can swim.
    The duck and the bird argue and argue. (363)

B. Elders advise us on matters. Elders have experience such as manners and marriage. They tell us how well they were brought up and the success they came across as a result of good manners. Elders tell us what to do when you want to get married, that is, making our future bright, and elders tell you how to behave in front of your in-laws. They say how people will treat you if you are polite and how people will treat you if you are not polite.

    Communication becomes easy after listening to their advice. Elders warn us against vulgar language. Elders have experienced bad or good. They warn us against bad and what bad leads to and how to get out of trouble when you're involved. Maybe they got involved in the same type of trouble.

    When it comes to religion and evidence of the past elders are a good source of evidence which enables us to write books containing information about the past. Even though some bits are distorted we get something on which to depend for historical events which even happened before we were born. In order to live happily we need manners from elders and from them we need money for education.

[Data supplied by Juliet Thondhlana] (364)

---

5. The word *such* is like *so* in having a variety of uses, but only some of these are used as a cohesive device. Explain how *such* is used in these examples. If it is a cohesive device, say what kind.

A. Chomsky is concerned in the first instance with describing the system of knowledge which speakers of a language have in their minds; such a description is called a grammar of that language (if it is fully explicit, a generative grammar). (365)

B. I got special permission to have three visits in the five days of my stay. We were hardly able to talk during these thirty-minute visits. All subjects were banned and every few minutes the warder in charge threatened me that the visit would be terminated if I 'discussed that subject' – whatever it was. I had missed David so much and had waited such a long time to visit him. (366)

C. Graver still was Patrick Cormack (C, Staffs S), a man of such majesty that even colleagues do not always appreciate quite how majestic he is. Unwilling to say anything as undignified as 'bluey', the name for servicemen's free mail, we had to guess what he meant by 'blue-letter forms'. (367)

D. Among rodents, species such as gophers that eat leaves or grass have smaller brains than those such as squirrels, which eat fruit, seeds and nuts. It is not precisely clear why there should be this relationship, but fruit, in general, is more difficult to find than leaves, and requires an animal to range further afield to acquire it. (368)

E. How do speakers of English acquire the Binding Principle? The answer, we now see, is that they do not acquire it at all – because it is in their heads to begin with. ... The principle is part of the grammar of English because the human brain is built in such a way that it could not be otherwise. The Binding Principle is part of what Chomsky calls Universal Grammar, a theory of 'our biological endowment', and this endowment places limits on what human languages can be like. (369)

Compare also the instances of *such* in examples 81, 106, 225 and 298.

6. [The examples in this exercise are taken from *The Trend*, July 1990, a trilingual English–French–German newsletter published by Telekurs AG, Zurich.] Cohesive devices are sometimes used differently in other languages than English. For instance, the ellipsis in this English example is not possible in French, which uses the reference item *le* instead:

> (370) Regional differences must be taken into account, and they will be [].
> ::
> *Les différences régionales doivent être prises en compte, et elles le seront.*

In this example, German uses the substitute *dabei* where English does not use any cohesive device:

> (371) The interdependence between a company's business activities, market conditions, and IT implementation strategies are clearly apparent. The manner of implementation depends on the type of technology, the available expertise, and the timing.
> ::
> *Die Interdependenzen zwischen Geschäftstätigkeit des Unternehmens, den Marktgegebenheiten und den Einsatzstrategien von Informationstechnologien sind klar zu erkennen. Ein kompetenter Einsatz ist dabei abhängig von der Art der Technologie, des Know-hows, und vom richtigen Zeitpunkt.*

(There are, of course, other differences between the English and German texts, such as the fact that *interdependence* is singular but *Interdependenzen* is plural. Here we are just concerned with differences in the use of cohesive devices.)

✎ Compare the use of cohesive devices in the following English text and its French and German translations.

> (372) What will the bank of the future be like?
>
> Banks all over the world are wondering what a successfully run financial institution will look like in the future. At present, the strong banks are designed as universal ones, either on the model of the Deutsche Bank or like the great Japanese finance houses. On the other hand the American banks have lost ground to competitors not only abroad, but also in important home markets, such as California. Moreover, the American banking system has been further weakened by the continuing savings bank crisis. Foreign banks too are increasingly moving away from the idea of operating as universal,

worldwide banks. Nor has there been any substantiation of the claim that operating in this way leads to returns of scale because of greater size. And so the universal banks are trying to operate on the home market as universal banks in all areas of banking activity, while being more selective in foreign territories.

(373) A quoi ressemblera la banque de demain?

Les banques du monde entier se demandent à quoi ressemblera l'institut financiel idéal de demain. Aujourd'hui, les banques puissantes sont des banques universelles, soit du type de la Deutsche Bank, soit du type des grands instituts financiers japonais. Les banques américaines, elles, perdent de terrain face à la concurrence, autant sur le marché international que dans certaines régions des USA comme la Californie. Le scandale des caisses d'épargne affaiblit encore le système financier américain. Mais les banques étrangères commencent aussi à hésiter à agir internationalement en tant que banques universelles. Le fait que les banques universelles profitent de gains cumulatifs provenant de leur situation est de plus en plus mis en doute. C'est pourquoi les banques internationales ont donc de plus en plus tendance à agir en tant que banques universelles sur le marché intérieur, et à se developper de façon plus sélective sur le marché international.

(374) Wie sieht die Bank der Zukunft aus?

Die Banken fragen sich weltweit, wie ein erfolgreich geführtes Finanzinstitut in der Zukunft aussehen wird. Heute sind die starken Banken als Universalbanken ausgestattet, entweder nach dem Vorbild der Deutschen Bank oder wie die grossen japanischen Finanzhäuser. Dagegen haben die amerikanischen Banken im Ausland, aber auch in wichtigen Heimmärkten wie Kalifornien, gegenüber der ausländischen Konkurrenz an Boden verloren. Zusätzlich geschwächt wird das amerikanische Finanzsystem durch die anhaltende Sparkassenkrise. Aber auch die ausländischen Banken kommen immer mehr vom Gedanken ab, weltweit als Universalbank zu agieren. Noch hat sich die Behauptung, dass globale Universalbanken durch ihre Grösse von Skalenerträgen profitieren können, nich bestätigt. Vermehrt versuchen die internationalen Banken deshalb, im Heimmarkt als

Universalbank in allen Banksparten tätig zu sein, und die Expansion ins Ausland selektiver zu strukturieren.

---

7. A text will sometimes indicate what kind of text it is. Such an indication will usually come early on, and can take a number of forms. One is the title: the words *textbook* or *prospectus* in titles such as *A textbook of translation* or *Sussex University Prospectus 1993/94* tell a reader what kind of text to expect. The preface of a book is often used for this purpose:

> (375) This is an exciting time for population genetics because it is becoming united with molecular biology. . . . This book is our attempt to convey the excitement and enthusiasm shared by our colleagues in the field.

> (376) In recent years there has been a change in emphasis in the content of GCE Advanced Level syllabuses in biological science. . . . It is with these changes in mind that this book has been written.

Magazines and newspapers often have words at the top of the page to indicate the type of material on that page. Such words include *Letters*, *Comment and Analysis*, *Talking Point*, *Advertisement* or *Advertiser's Announcement*, *Profile*, *Short Story* and *Foreign News*.

✎ Look through the texts in this book and pick out the ones where you are fairly sure what kind of text each is. Try to explain what it is about the text that makes you so sure.

FURTHER READING

COHESION

The first nine chapters of this book draw heavily on M. Halliday and R. Hasan, *Cohesion in English* (London, Longman, 1976). This is not always an easy book to follow: a shorter, slightly modified version of the same material can be found in M. Halliday, *An Introduction to Functional Grammar* (second edition, London, Edward Arnold, 1994), especially see Chapter 7, 'Above the clause: the clause complex' and Chapter 9, 'Around the clause: cohesion'. Short summaries of Halliday and Hasan's system can be found in A. Hartley, *Linguistics for Language Learners* (London, Macmillan, 1982), Chapter 10, 'Text structure'; H. Jackson, *Analyzing English* (Oxford, Pergamon, 1980), Chapter 15, 'Text 2: Cohesion'; and M. Baker, *In Other Words: A Coursebook on Translation* (London, Routledge, 1992), Chapter 6, 'Cohesion'. For criticism of this approach see P. Carrell, 'Cohesion is not coherence', *TESOL Quarterly* 16.4, 1982, pp. 479–88.

CLAUSE RELATIONS

Chapter 10 draws on the 'clause relation' approach to discourse analysis, set out notably in E. Winter, 'A clause relational approach to English texts: a study of some predictive items in written discourse', *Instructional Science* 6.1, 1977, pp. 1–92; and E. Winter, *Toward a Contextual Grammar of English* (London, George Allen & Unwin, 1982). More approachable accounts of clause relations are M. Jordan, *Rhetoric of Everyday English Texts* (London, George Allen & Unwin, 1984); M. Hoey, *On the Surface of Discourse* (London, George Allen & Unwin, 1983); and M. Hoey, *Patterns of Lexis in Text* (Oxford, Oxford University Press, 1991). An interesting paper in this framework is A. Tadros, 'Predictive Categories in University Textbooks', *English for Specific Purposes* 8, 1989, pp. 17–31, on which Further Exercise No. 3 is based. See also A. Tadros, 'Predictive Categories in Expository Text', in M. Coulthard (ed.), *Advances in Written Text Analysis* (London, Routledge, 1994), pp. 69–82.

Two good general introductions to text and discourse analysis are aimed in particular at language teachers, and therefore take a practical approach: G. Cook, *Discourse* (Oxford, Oxford University Press, 1989); and M. McCarthy, *Discourse Analysis for Language Teachers* (Cambridge, Cambridge University Press, 1991).

For more wide-ranging and theory-based introductions to the subject, try R. de Beaugrande and W. Dressler, *Introduction to Text Linguistics* (London, Longman, 1981); and G. Brown and W. Yule, *Discourse Analysis* (Cambridge, Cambridge University Press, 1983). The bibliographies in these four books will point you towards more specialised works in the field.

GENERAL TEXTBOOKS

INDEX